BARBARA L. JOHNSON has more than 25 years'
experience as a book collector and sometime
bookseller. Her research has taken her to
several countries on three continents to in-
terview book restorers, librarians, private collectors, world-famous booksellers, and book
scouts.

Book Scouting

How to Turn Your Love for Books into Profit

BARBARA L. JOHNSON

Photographs by Richard A. Jasany
Illustrations by Raymond J. Rossin

A SPECTRUM BOOK

PRENTICE-HALL, INC., *Englewood Cliffs, New Jersey* 07632

Library of Congress Cataloging in Publication Data

JOHNSON, BARBARA L
  Book scouting.

  (A Spectrum Book)
  Includes index.
    1. Antiquarian booksellers.   2. Book collecting.
  I. Title.
  Z286.A55J64   070.5068'8   80-17336
  ISBN 0-13-080077-5
  ISBN 0-13-080069-4 (pbk.)

10 9 8 7 6 5 4 3 2 1

Editorial/production supervision
and interior design by Eric Newman
Art production by Marie Alexander
Cover design and illustration by Michael Aron
Manufacturing buyer: Cathie Lenard

PRENTICE-HALL INTERNATIONAL, INC., *London*
PRENTICE-HALL OF AUSTRALIA PTY. LIMITED, *Sydney*
PRENTICE-HALL OF CANADA, LTD., *Toronto*
PRENTICE-HALL OF INDIA PRIVATE LIMITED, *New Delhi*
PRENTICE-HALL OF JAPAN, INC., *Tokyo*
PRENTICE-HALL OF SOUTHEAST ASIA PTE. LTD., *Singapore*
WHITEHALL BOOKS LIMITED, *Wellington, New Zealand*

To my husband, David,
who says he can never lose me in any city in the world.
All he has to do is make the rounds of the bookshops,
and in one of them, I'll turn up.

Contents

Acknowledgments

My sincere appreciation goes to the following book people who contributed their time and knowledge to the making of this book:

Robert Beerbohm, Owner
Best of Two Worlds

Johanna Goldschmid, Curator, Special Collections
San Francisco Public Library

Robert C. Halsey, Owner
Jabberwock Books

The late Harry Hartman
Harry Hartman Booksellers, Inc.

Margaret M. Herbring, Owner
Philip W. Townshend Somerville,
Antiquarian Bookman
Morningsun Rare Books

Warren R. Howell, President
John Howell—Books

Robert L. Lucas, Book Restorer and Conservator

Maurice F. Powers, President
Ean S. Richards, Vice President
California Book Auction Galleries

Rose and Donald Sharp, Owners/Managers
The Albatross Book Store

Rosalie Spellman, Librarian
Aberdeen, Washington, Public Library

Carol Spencer, Owner/Manager
Sunset Bookstore

Diane Vasica and Gerald Webb, Co-Owners
Arkadyan Books and Prints

A Note to the Reader: In order not to interrupt the flow of the text, no special attempt has been made to define technical terms used in the text. Chapter 9 contains a glossary that begins on page 142.

I

Bookworms Make Good Book Scouts

I F YOU LOVE BOOKS and like to read, if you've been
called a bookworm because you often have your
nose in a book, and if you like to browse in libraries
and bookshops, you've probably stored up a lot of
knowledge about books. Now there may be a way you
can use that stored-up knowledge to earn some money.
It's possible to turn your love for books into profit by
becoming a book scout.

Book scouting is a way to be a bookworm, to spend
time around books, and to earn money while doing it.

Book scouts, sometimes called *runners*, because
they do a lot of running after books, are people who
seek out and buy collectible and readily salable books
from low-priced outlets and then resell them to dealers
and collectors for a profit. A book scout is a speculator
in rare, old, and used resalable books.

THE BOOK AUDIENCE

There are two distinct classifications of book scouts—
the scouts who speculate in high-priced, rare, and
ANTIQUARIAN books and those who buy and sell
secondhand books available at a lower price.

Of course, the top earners in the field are scouts
who deal in rare and antiquarian books. These people
risk larger amounts of capital to buy books, but they
nearly always sell their volumes for a higher profit than
those who deal in secondhand books. Scouts who
handle only rare books sell at auctions, to antiquarian
dealers, or directly to well-to-do collectors. A vast
amount of background knowledge and experience is

needed to be a successful scout in the rare-book field. *This text does not deal with this kind of book scout.*

The second type of book scout is the one who deals in used books that are less rare and less costly. *This book is addressed to those people who would like to get into this modestly priced book scouting field.*

Although book scouts who buy and sell lower-priced volumes may never make vast amounts of money, they usually find that part of their reward comes from the many book lovers they meet and keep as friends and the joy they derive in the work itself. Many collectors, wanting to earn a little money to buy books for themselves, retired people who only want to work part-time, or students who need a little extra income are three examples of the kinds of people who find this type of scouting ideal for their employment needs.

HOW TO GET STARTED
AS A BOOK SCOUT

Becoming a book scout is not as complicated as getting into many other trades. Bookworms will find that they have already acquired some of the knowledge they'll need, and some of the skills they'll be using can be learned on the job. Of course, beginners can expect to make a few mistakes in buying and selling when they start out, but any loss suffered from these errors can be considered money well spent as a part of their education. Mistakes are one way of learning.

Another way a beginning book scout can learn the trade is to serve an apprenticeship as a clerk in a used-book shop for a few months. Being an apprentice takes time, but it is less costly than the trial-and-error method of learning. Clerking in a shop not only allows you to earn while you learn; it also offers these other advantages:

√A chance to gain experience working with store owners who know sales skills

√A way to learn customer buying habits

√An opportunity to see, firsthand, the type of books that are in greatest demand

√A way to see how books are priced

Of course, it may not always be possible to find a job in a bookshop or to be able to spare the time needed to serve an apprenticeship, so it is good that book scouting knowledge can be acquired by the trial-and-error method. Learning by doing takes a little longer, and errors cost; but the end knowledge is the same.

A BOOK SCOUT'S QUALIFICATIONS

There are several other qualifications a beginning book scout would do well to have besides sales skills. The personality traits that follow are also most important.

A Book Scout Should Love Books

People without great interest in books would probably not do well as scouts. Being a book scout is living with books on your mind every day while you spend long

Working in a used-book shop, waiting on trade, seeing what people buy are the best ways to learn pricing and what will sell.

hours poring over dusty boxes of books, prowling streets in search of garage sales, and going to junkshops trying to track down salable volumes. Book scouts talk to people about the books they are trying to sell, and they listen to the want lists of books that people are trying to find—not an ideal routine if you don't love books.

A Book Scout Should Always Be Willing to Learn

Pricing and demands change constantly in the book world, so it is not enough to learn once what types of books are salable and what they will bring on the market; this information must be updated continually. A scout should be willing to turn in old information for new data to keep sales skills current.

A Book Scout Should Have a Good Memory

Developing a good memory is of primary importance to success. When scouts are out looking for salable books, they should be able to keep customer want lists and current book values in their heads and not have to take time out to refer to lists and notes.

A Book Scout Should Like People

Buying and selling books call for constant contact with dealers and others who have books for sale and with customers you wish to interest in buying what you have to offer. Scouts who have pleasing personalities and who genuinely like people will make more sales and will find that more customers come back to trade with them on a regular basis.

Liking people is one of the most important qualifications for becoming a good book scout.

A Book Scout Should Have a Natural Sense of Book Value

Whether book scouts are dealing in ten-dollar books or fifty-dollar volumes, they need the judgment to decide what books they can resell at a profit and which ones they should turn down. Part of this ability to judge value comes with experience, but it is fair to say that part of it is also an innate sense.

WHAT TO INVEST IN TO GET STARTED

Being a book scout has it all over going into many other types of businesses that call for set hours and a large financial investment. Here are some details about what a book scout really needs to invest in to get started.

A Scout's Bookshop Can Be a Box
of Books in the Trunk of an
Automobile or a Briefcase Packed
with Three or Four Volumes

A book scout doesn't need to invest in real estate or pay rent. For decades, people who love books have been cashing in their life savings and setting themselves up in quaint, snug little bookshops. Eventually, many of these people quietly go broke. A shop means overhead and immobility, bills for upkeep, light, and heat. Scouts who carry their few books directly to the customer save this high overhead. Bookshops also tie their owners down, so they can't be out hunting for books—the very lifeblood of their business. Bookshop owners who wait for buyers to come to them may lose both time and money, for those buyers may never get around to showing up. Scouts have the best of two worlds—no overhead and easy mobility.

A Book Scout Needs to Buy Only
a Few Volumes to Get Started

A book scout doesn't need a large inventory as does a bookshop owner who has empty shelves to fill. A few good books that will sell fast can land interested customers for a scout and the profits to buy more books. Fast turnover, not a large inventory, is the secret to success.

Book Scouts May Choose
Their Own Hours

Scouts can work all day, every day, or they can pursue scouting in their spare time. Scouts can choose to work as little as one day a week, or every day if they like. All kinds of people have started scouting in the corners of their time. Retired people, bored by idleness, find book scouting a happy way to return to the mainstream of business. Mothers with only a few hours of free time can work as book scouts while their children are in school. Many people who have full-time jobs start out book scouting to earn a little extra cash, and sometimes they end up changing careers by becoming full-time book scouts. Many collectors are now-and-then book scouts who purchase good buys when they see them and resell the books to earn a little extra money for their own collections. Of course, the more time people devote to scouting, the more money they are likely to earn; but unlike bookshop owners, who must keep open for set hours nearly every day, book scouts are free to work when they please.

BOOK SCOUTS ARE NEEDED

People nearly everywhere have awakened to the fact that old books are escalating in value. Book collecting, in addition to being a fascinating hobby, has now become a field for investors. When one considers that the appreciation rate of old books now equals, if not surpasses, that of real estate, it is not surprising that speculators have moved into the field. Today, investors are buying books in all kinds of categories—from old dime novels to comic books. Victorian romances, paperback Westerns, and even old vanity-press poetry books in fine bindings are being sold. Books in almost any category, in good condition, are being purchased for speculation. Not all are appreciating in value like rare books, but it would be well to remember that the kinds of books your grandmother may have bundled up for junk are now bringing bids at auctions. Almost every kind of old book is appreciating in value; some types, of course, will make you rich faster than others.

Regardless of why people are collecting old books, the fact remains that the demand is soaring. The book-collecting business has become a multimillion-dollar-per-year operation. Evidence of this increase in interest can be seen in the fact that periodicals dealing with the book trade have nearly doubled their subscription lists in the last few years. And even more indicative of interest in the field are the hundreds of bidders and onlookers who regularly attend book auctions.

Farmers and field hands are beginning to collect books, and so are plumbers and politicians. Book buyers are coming from all walks of life. It's not just the wealthy who collect books anymore; librarians, teachers, students, parents, and even children are collecting.

The upswing in demand is creating a like demand for book scouts. Many beginning collectors who do not

Anyone who has recently attended a book auction can have little doubt that the old-book trade is booming.

know where to look for the volumes on their want lists are happy to rely on a scout to seek them out. Additionally, many bookshop owners are now too busy to go on buying trips and welcome scouts who bring in good, salable volumes.

BOOK SCOUTING
PITFALLS

It would not be fair to present only one side of the book scouting story—the success side. Anyone working as a book scout for any time at all would point out a few common job drawbacks.

√To make good money, books scouts have to work hard. Book scouts aren't called *runners* without reason.

√Like any set of customers, book buyers have been known to
   Order books and change their minds
   Give bad checks
   Handle delicate merchandise excessively
   Offer to pay less than the product is worth

√People who sell to book scouts have been known to
   Overcharge
   Fail to deliver promised orders
   Misrepresent their product
   Change their mind about a price
   Withdraw books previously offered for sale

Book scouting, like any business, has drawbacks, but many of the obvious pitfalls can be avoided.

A BOOK SCOUT TEST

You may agree with everything that has been said about the joy of being around books, about the increasing demand for old volumes, and about the need for book scouts but still be in doubt about whether you have the necessary talent and temperament to succeed in the field. There's one sure way to test yourself and find out if you'll make a good book scout before you commit yourself fully. You can try the six-step test that follows and see for yourself whether or not you can turn your love for books into profit.

Complete each step before going on to the next.

1. Read this book through to the end. Pay special attention to the sections that tell about the types of books to buy and where to sell them.

2. Personally check out all the book-supply sources in your area that are recommended in Chapter 3.

3. Using the recommendations outlined in Chapter 4, buy three books in good condition.

4. In a minimum amount of time, clean and restore these books, using the simple home remedies described in Chapter 5.

5. Find the best-paying customers for your three books, using the guidelines offered in Chapter 6.

6. Try out the basic sales techniques, outlined in Chapter 7, to sell your books at a profit.

When you have completed this procedure, ask yourself if you enjoyed the experience and if you would like to reinvest your profits in more books to try to make additional sales. If your answer is yes to all these questions, it is safe for you to decide to give book scouting a full-scale try. Turn the page, and you are on your way to a new adventure!

2

Books in Demand

T HE MOST IMPORTANT QUESTION book scouts can ask themselves before they buy is: "Will this book resell for a profit in a minimum amount of time?" Never buy a book unless you can answer yes to that question. Judging a book's salability, however, takes experience, skill, a good knowledge of current market conditions, and a gut feeling about what makes a book worth owning. Skill comes with experience, but the gut feeling is inborn. Most people who are avid readers and who love books have that ability to judge value. Some book scouts ask themselves, "Would I like to own this book?" and if the answer is yes, they buy it.

However, experience in working with books should never be discounted. Part of knowing what will sell is knowing who does the buying. In this chapter we discuss various types of buyers—ranging all the way from collectors to other book scouts—and then we list the types of books that interest these different buyers. One of the best clues to understanding *what* people buy is understanding *why* they buy, so we start there.

WHY PEOPLE BUY BOOKS

There are dozens of reasons why people buy books besides the most obvious one—to read them. A few of the most common reasons follow:

√To study the literature and writing of a past age.

√For the joy of the chase that is involved in tracking down a rare or unusual book.

√To accumulate a collection to pass on as a family heirloom or to give as a gift to a museum or library.

√To restore neglected volumes. Buyers may be restoration experts who enjoy the work and who have a real desire to save books that might otherwise be lost.

√For their beauty. Beauty can take many forms in book art—all the way from the finely hand-tooled volume to a paper-covered Western novel with a picture of the hero emblazoned across its cover.

√For an interest in book production. Some people collect the work of famous printers or binders.

√As occupational tools. Some people buy reference material to help them in their work. Lawyers, doctors, ministers, and many different professionals have working book collections.

√To supplement a hobby. People who are interested in sailing buy books about boats; those who are interested in gardens buy books about landscaping.

√As an investment or hedge against inflation. People who buy books for investment purposes are often looking for first editions, fine bindings, AMERICANA, or rare manuscripts, but you may find some who are interested in old comic books.

An important thing to remember is that to profit in book scouting, match the books you have for sale to the people who are interested in buying them. For example, old and unusual cookbooks should first be offered to the culinary experts who might be most apt to buy them. It follows that the more you know about why people buy certain books, the more successful you will be in finding books that sell. Never pass up an opportunity to talk with buyers, whether they be collectors or speculators or just readers.

DEALERS AS CUSTOMERS

There are many classifications of dealers who buy and sell books for profit. All of them can be considered book scout customers. Some scouts prefer to sell to dealers exclusively and have one or two outlets where they take all their books. This arrangement offers the advantage of a ready market once the scout builds up a relationship. However, this marketing method has a drawback, too. Scouts who sell to other dealers are not likely to get as much for their books as they would if they sold directly to a private customer. But beginning scouts lacking contact with very many buyers may want to try to sell their finds to dealers.

Several classifications of dealers who may be ready buyers follow:

Specialist Dealers

These dealers sell a special kind of collectible book. Some specialists, for example, deal only in first editions or in INCUNABULA. If you are lucky enough to come across such a book but lack the experience to sell it yourself, you would do well to offer it to a dealer who specializes.

Mail-Quote Dealers

These dealers send out lists and catalogues with descriptions and prices of what they have for sale. Some mail-quote dealers advertise in trade periodicals, both the books that are wanted and those for sale.

Used-Book-Shop Dealers

Used-book-shop owners buy most of their books from people who bring them in by the boxload. This is a low-paying market and may be a last resort for books that a scout cannot sell elsewhere.

Consignment Booksellers and Auction Houses

These outlets sell for a percentage of the sale price. Auction houses commonly charge 10 percent to both buyer and seller.

Antiquarian Dealers

These are the top specialists in the bookselling world. Many will buy only rare books and manuscripts.

Other Book Scouts

If you have a book that another scout has a customer for and you have failed to sell to higher-paying outlets, sell to the scout, take less profit, and free your capital.

BOOKS THAT SELL

In the more moderately priced book field, there are several classifications of books that sell more readily than others. Beginning books scouts would do well to learn what types of books these are, so they can be alert for them when they are out on a book search.

Furniture Books
or Cocktail-Table Books

These are the large, pictorial volumes that many people leave out for show. Few of these books are ever heavily read, so they are apt to be in good condition. However, it is wise to look at the covers to see if anyone has used them for a cocktail coaster. This is a common fate for this type of book and, of course, devalues it.

Large Books

Some people who buy used books just want to get the most book for their money. If a large book is at all interesting, it will sell more readily than a slim volume.

Cookbooks

Many people who do not consider themselves book collectors do collect cookbooks to read and use.

Art Books

Narrative and critical catalogs of art exhibitions and collections generally sell well. The more lavishly a book is illustrated, the more it will bring in price, just as it did when it was new.

Music Books

Historical accounts of great performances, ranging from opera to jazz, meet with enthusiastic acceptance.

Those oversized pictorial books that people are fond of leaving out on cocktail tables are always on the want lists of used-book-shop owners.

Reference Books

Dictionaries, thesauri, or instant spelling books are always on the want lists of used-book dealers, who get many more calls for them than they can fill.

BOOKS THAT
DON'T SELL

Don't be attracted to a book with a shiny cover, one that is in new condition, or even one that is lavishly illustrated if it falls into any of the categories that follow. These are the books that most secondhand-bookstore dealers would probably turn down.

Textbooks
This applies to all textbooks unless they are current and offered at a school bookstore.

Book-Club Fiction More Than
Six Months Old
Even if the book was a best-seller when it came out, very few dealers want to take a chance that they will find a buyer who hasn't already read it.

Books on Political Science
Yesterday's top candidates and issues are today's dead books.

Biography
The life stories of forgotten sports figures, obscure politicians, and unimportant movie stars sell very poorly.

Most Hardback Novels
Today's readers prefer paperbacks, which they recycle for more books.

Last Year's Crop of Diet Books

Diet books, beauty guides, exercise and body-shaping books, and other self-improvement books that were last year's fads are this year's rejects.

Most Vanity-Press Books

Most books that authors paid to have published, unfortunately, were probably not good enough to find a paying publisher and are therefore poor reading.

Anthologies of Poetry, Short Stories, or Essays

A subject that is explored in every aspect in a full book is more popular than many short themes collected under one cover.

Books in a Foreign Language

One of the reasons bookshop owners do not like to buy foreign-language books is that they cannot read them for content to judge if they are interesting.

Books in Poor Condition

Used-bookshop dealers cannot spend time repairing books that are damaged or badly worn.

WHAT BOOKS COLLECTORS ARE LOOKING FOR

The key to the best profits in book scouting is to be able to spot those books that are in demand by collectors who will pay top price for what they want.

Collectors can be divided into several different categories according to the type of books they collect. Some buy books in more than one category, but roughly, collectors can be grouped as follows:

Collectors of Antiquarian and Rare Books

Under this group come the buyers who collect:

√ First editions

√ Private-press fine editions

√ Americana

√ Author-autographed editions

√ Fine bindings

√ Antiquarian and rare books

√ Books with fine plates

√ Fore-edge books

√ Limited editions and other rarities, including books with errors

Collectors of Fad Books

People who have fad collections are of every age and budget range. Nostalgia is one of the factors dominating today's fad collections, as can be clearly seen by this list of books popular with fad collectors:

√ Victorian novels

√ Westerns

√ Mystery

√ Science fiction

√ Comic books

Comic books are becoming a very hot sales item with an up-and-coming group of young collectors. Some stores are now specializing in them.

Some fad collectors also collect books that have been banned or suppressed.

One-Author or One-Subject Collectors

Some collectors want only the books of one particular author. All editions and all books that one author produced make up such collections.

One-subject collections, such as fishing, railroads, and costumes, are quite popular.

Fine-Craftsmanship Collectors

Some books are collected, not for the text or author, but for some special adornment that is an intrinsic part of the volume. Many of these adornments, some even of gold and silver, add greatly to the value of the book. Unique craftsmanship in binding, tooling, and printing are also among those features that are being sought by craftsmanship collectors.

Other book adornments popular with collectors are:

- *Bookplates.* Early plates were hand-painted and were a work of art in themselves.
- *Armorial bindings.* Books ornamented with crests on either front or back covers were first in fashion as early as 1490. These early books usually belonged to kings or men of great wealth. Later editions contained school crests, coats of arms from clubs and colleges, and special library crests.
- *Panorama picture books.* Some books have fragile, illustrated plates that stand up in layered dimensions like old-fashioned valentines when the book is opened. Many children's books were illustrated in this manner.
- *Jeweled covers.* Some books are actually studded with precious gems.
- *Books with silver or gold hinges or bosses.*

Should you be lucky enough to find a panorama picture book like this one, in good condition, you have a readily salable item.

√*Books with unusual bindings.* Books that have been bound in fur, silk, hand embroidery, and rare types of leather are sought by many collectors.

Collectors of Books of Unusual Size

Books in unusual sizes are the subject of some collections. Two extremes in size are as follows:

√*Miniature books.* Any book that measures under three inches in height is classified as a miniature. Some tiny books are perfect in every detail, beautifully bound, and printed with legible type. Fine

Miniature books are in demand both by collectors and as gift items.

miniatures are becoming rare and command a good price.

Folio books. Very large books, originally those that measured 17 by 20 inches, are known as folio books. These were made by folding a piece of standard book paper only once.

If you are lucky enough to find collectible types of books when you are scouting about, and they are in fairly good condition, you won't lose by buying them. It follows that the more you know about why books are collected, the more successful you will be in finding books that sell. Never pass up an opportunity to talk with collectors, and make every attempt to see and study fine books. If you've never seen a FORE-EDGE, for example, or aren't sure what a VELLUM book looks like, you should consider it part of your education to find out. The glossary included in Chapter 9 will help you define terms, but you should make an attempt to see all types of rare books firsthand.

WHERE TO LEARN
MORE ABOUT BOOKS

Book lessons are around you every day. Every place you go, look at books, study how they are made and what they cost, and look to see who owns them; these people are your prospective customers.

The most obvious place to look at books is in a library, but there are many other places as well. Here is a list of places to go to study book art:

✓ Visit antiquarian, secondhand, and new-book shops. Look at books that are featured, note their prices, and observe who is buying them.

✓ Attend a book fair if you live near a community that has one. Talk with buyers and collectors. Fairs

Visit the nearest public library that has a rare-book collection. Study what the bindings, the paper, and the printing look like in fine old volumes.

are a good place to see what new collecting fads are surfacing.

√Visit book clubs and talk with collectors.

√Go to book auctions, read the catalogues, and watch the bidding.

√Read trade periodicals to find out what books are appearing on the want lists.

√Visit great collections whenever you travel. You might consider planning your vacation around a book tour. The more you see of fine books, the better your eye will be for buying. (See Chapter 9 for a list of places to see fine collections.)

Where to Find Resalable Books

A MERE TWENTY YEARS AGO, book bargains could be found in every secondhand bookshop, and boxes of beautiful old volumes were stacked in attics and hidden away on back shelves just waiting to be found. This is no longer true, because many of those books are now in the hands of collectors, and an ever-increasing number of people are looking for the few fine volumes that are still undiscovered.

Collectors, dealers, decorators, and people who just like to read are on the trail of old books. Many of these people have a pretty good idea of what makes a book valuable and worth buying. There is a lot of good information currently available concerning book value. Most people need only go to their local library to find it.

Added to the problem that more knowledgeable people are looking for books is the fact that many of the really fine and rare volumes have already been found. Contrary to what many people believe, there never was a large supply of fine books. Quantity has always been limited, and considering all the destructive things people can think of to do to books, it is a wonder that any have survived dryness, dampness, fire, and flood. But this does not mean that a diligent book scout can't make a modest living dealing in volumes that are less than rare and not costly.

A book scout who aims at a more modest market still has a wide range of customers. Small used-book stores are always ready to buy good reading copies. Collectors with limited budgets and modestly priced collections are just as enthusiastic to buy their type of book as their wealthier counterparts. And some libraries are becoming prospective customers, because limited funds often cause library committees to seek good used books.

The market is there, but once again, the competition is too. More people are examining their used books carefully and selling them themselves, at garage sales or to used-book shops. More collectors are doing their own buying, and more small book dealers are themselves out beating the bushes for good used books. Still, a book scout can succeed in finding bargains where others fail by being in the right place at the right *time*. A big secret in finding books is to know *when* to look, in addition to knowing *where* to look.

WHY TIMING IS
IMPORTANT

Though many people do not associate timing with being a good book scout, *when* you get to a book sale is today's most important element of success. Timing is of primary importance when looking for books at fairs, auctions, bazaars, flea markets, and even neighborhood garage sales. To get the best books offered, you need to be where they are offered ahead of your competition. No wise dealer or eager collector is going to leave a share of the bargains for you, just as you shouldn't leave any bargains behind where you have looked. Get to a sale spot first to get the best.

WHERE TO LOOK FOR
BOOK BARGAINS

Under Your Own Roof

Before you go off to a sale or downtown to your favorite thrift shop in search of books, look for salable volumes right under your own roof. Yes, your own bookshelf is the place to start your search. Chances are, you've accumulated a good number of volumes that you have no intention of ever looking at again. Cull those books out, and look them over with a new eye—a book scout's eye. Maybe you inherited your grandmother's bird books, and they never appealed to you, so you put them away in a back closet. To a book scout, they may look different. They may look like a sure sale.

Dust off your finds, read up on the market, and have a try at selling. Those books under your own roof just might bring you the cash you need to get started in business.

Your Family's Books

After you've surveyed all the books under your own roof, the next logical step is to have a look at the books of other members of your family. Maybe your Aunt Mary has a stack of cookbooks she's tired of storing but doesn't want to bother to try to sell. Offer her a fair price for them, and she may be glad to have you haul them away.

Maybe your cousin Shirley has outgrown her collection of dog books and was thinking of giving them to a neighbor. Offer to buy them; she'll probably be pleased to make a few dollars she wasn't anticipating.

But don't start a family rift by thinking that all relatives are going to want to sell you their books. Some probably wouldn't think of parting with one of their volumes, particularly if they are collectors.

You may convince some members of your family to help you search elsewhere. This broadens your buying territory. Certainly others will have friends you don't know, and they will very likely travel to places you don't go. Try to interest your aunts, uncles, and cousins in asking around for salable books. If these helpers turn up anything worth selling, offer them a share of the profits. Don't take on any helpers as employees, however, or you'll have a lot of official paperwork to worry about. (This type of detail is fully explained in Chapter 8.)

After you've looked over all of your family's books, it's time to go out into the world. But don't go too far. The next logical place is your own neighborhood. Once you move outside the family on your book search, timing plays a much more important part in success.

Your Neighbor's Books

Thou shalt not covet thy neighbor's books, but he or she may want to sell a few. There's no harm done by asking. If you don't ask first, some other book scout probably will. Call on your neighbors, and tell them honestly that you are interested in buying old books to resell. Ask if they have any books that they are no longer interested in and might want to sell.

However, if your neighbor drags out a few cartons of old paperbacks or book club editions, don't feel obligated to buy, or you'll shoot all your profits for the week. Tell your neighbors truthfully that you don't think you could resell the volumes at a profit. Thank them for their time, and clear out.

Never tell your neighbors in advance what kinds of books you are looking for. This only gives them a chance to judge the books they have and decide you may not be interested. Always offer to look at whatever they might be willing to sell. *You* decide whether the books they have are resalable.

Don't give up on neighborhoods just because nothing turns up at first. Wait until a "for sale" sign goes up in the area; better still, when you *first* hear that your neighbors are planning to move, get right over there and ask if they have any books they don't want to pack and transport. People who are moving may be more willing to part with some of their better books than to pay to move them. Books are heavy, and people who have to move often sell off parts of their libraries. Here again, timing is very important. Get to your neighbor *before* everyone else has a chance to pick over what isn't going along on the moving van.

Garage Sales

A garage sale is usually the last stopping-off place for unwanted possessions before charity thrift shops or the city dump gets them. If you don't go to a garage sale with high hopes of finding valuable books, you won't come home disappointed. Once every twenty times or so, you may find a book worth buying, but this will be the exception rather than the rule. There are good reasons for this absence of bargains.

First, even before neighbors hear of a garage sale, friends and family members may have culled out any valuable books. Second, if you don't get to the sale at the opening gun, other buyers will have grabbed up anything of value. Here again, see how important timing is?

Here is a random list of the types of books you are likely to find at the average garage sale that really aren't resalable:

√*Reader's Digest Condensed Books*
√Book club editions
√Torn and marked children's books
√Gothic paperbacks
√Mystery paperbacks
√Old magazines

Don't let this dismal list stop you from going to garage sales. Occasionally, you may find a slim leather volume of poetry, a nicely illustrated art book, or an unusual cookbook that will make your trip worthwhile. But get to such sales when they open, or don't go at all.

Flea Markets

Flea markets are usually like vast garage sales; they just involve more people and more junk. Some people who sell at flea markets are junk scouts and make it a full-time business. As a rule, the books you will find at flea markets will be of about the same caliber as those at garage sales. However, there is always a chance that you may uncover something in good condition that is resalable. Make it a policy to stop at flea markets (early in the day), and look over those long tables of books with a quick eye.

Book bargains still turn up at flea markets now and then, so don't pass one by without stopping for a quick look.

Junkshops and Charity
Thrift Stores

Some thrift shops are nothing more than garage sales under a permanent roof. Thrift shops (especially charity ones) often get the leftovers from garage sales. Many of these small shops are the dumping ground for unwanted and nearly unsaleable items. Almost all thrift shops have a shelf or a carton or two of books for sale. Here, again, you are likely to find the same tired collection of cheap editions, old magazines, and paperbacks you passed up at garage sales, but with a little practice you can learn to survey a shelf or to pore over a carton in a few seconds. The longer you scout, the faster your eye will become.

Of course, some charity thrift shops do occasionally receive cartons of beautiful volumes from wealthy donors. Sometimes when an estate is broken up, books are cast into a donation box. In this way, some resalable books do find their way into thrift shops. Don't pass a shop by if you happen to be in the neighborhood. It takes only a few minutes to check out what's there.

Even if you don't see anything on the shelf, if you can talk your way into the back room where the unmarked items are kept, you'll have first choice on book donations.

Before leaving, give the proprietor your card, and ask to be called if any books in good condition come in. If the shop shows any promise of producing something salable, put a notation in your card file, and call the proprietor from time to time to see if any large donations have arrived.

Church and Charity Bazaars

Almost every bazaar has a book table. Sometimes people give better books to their church than they would offer to a thrift shop, and bazaar books are usually reasonably priced; this combination makes for good scouting.

Of course, some of the books won't be in any better condition or of any better caliber than those you find at garage sales and thrift shops. The secret to getting the best books at bazaars is to be the first one to look over the offerings. There are several ways to do this.

1. If the bazaar happens to be sponsored by *your* church or by a charitable organization *you* are a member of, volunteer to donate your services. Be the first to offer to work at the book table. This gives you the chance to be the first purchaser. Be sure to give the fair and going price for any volume you select and maybe even an extra donation for being the first to choose, and the bazaar committee won't be too likely to object.

2. If a neighbor's or friend's church is having a bazaar, ask that person to look over the books donated and to save those in good condition for you. Explain the types of books you are looking for, or type out a short want list giving general descriptions of such books. Again, when you buy, make a donation for the privilege of having the first choice.

3. If you can't volunteer and you don't know someone working at a bazaar, be at the front of the line on bazaar

day. If there are a lot of interested dealers in line, the good volumes will be picked out in a very few minutes. A fast eye and hand will help you here. You'll see dealers scoop up an armload of books as they come running up to a table. They'll hold the volumes until they have had a chance to look them over. If you're competing with this type of dealer, you may have to resort to this kind of action, too, if you expect to get any bargains.

Never waste your time going to a bazaar late in the day. The rule of thumb in book sales of any kind is to get in ahead of time if you can; if not, get there when the doors open.

If you do not find any salable volumes at a bazaar, this may be because all the good books have been offered to auction houses. Some organizations are now making a practice of pulling out their better books and not selling them at bazaars. Before you waste a lot of time waiting in line to get into a bazaar, try to find out if all books donated are being offered.

Used-Book Shops

Those vast old bookshops where volumes are shelved to the ceiling and spilling out of boxes stacked around the floor offer an exciting challenge, but don't let the profusion of books confuse you. The fact that a shop is a labyrinth of narrow passageways crowded on either side with every variety of book does not mean that the owner doesn't know what the stock is worth. Don't get the idea that such an intricate maze is without policy or that everything is necessarily a bargain. This kind of organized confusion can lead shoppers into thinking that they are stepping back in time and getting bargains from another era when, in reality, the books are actually at the current market price. Use your judgment and pricing knowledge in this kind of shop as well as anywhere else.

Used-book shops offer an exciting challenge, but a book scout needs good pricing knowledge to decide whether a book is a bargain that will resell for a profit.

You can also expect that books you buy in most bookshops are going to be more expensive than those you find for yourself in attics, garage sales, and bazaars. The book you buy from a shop has the cost of overhead tacked on. For example, if you pay one dollar for a book in a bookstore and take that book down the street to sell it to another dealer, you will probably only be offered fifty cents for it. The second dealer has to make the same profit the first one did.

There are two ways you may find bargains in a used-book shop: First, you may buy at a sale where shop owners are clearing out certain types of stock, such as religious books, children's books, or some other special type of book they no longer plan to carry. When a bookshop is moving to a new location or going out of business, you again may find bargains, so always be alert for sales.

The second way you may find a real bargain is when a book has been accidentally misplaced and you are lucky enough to find it. Sometimes browsers pull volumes from the shelves and replace them carelessly; books may be pushed behind the front row and remain hidden for long periods of time. Good resalable books that might otherwise have been purchased by other scouts and dealers sometimes get passed by this way. Learn to run your hand behind the rows of books on deep shelves to see if any treasures are lurking there. Climb up on stools and ladders, and check top shelves for overlooked volumes. These high-up shelves are the most often neglected.

Antiquarian Bookshops

It is always a pleasure for a book lover to visit an antiquarian bookshop where the books are kept in orderly rows and are well cared for. Antiquarian dealers bid for, and get, the cream of the old-book crop. Therefore, it stands to reason that prices in such shops will be high. However, if you have a customer who doesn't wish to take time to do a search for a certain rare volume, you may find yourself checking antiquarian bookshops. If you find what you are after, you may win the good will of that customer for other sales. In addition, you will probably find your foray into this world of costlier volumes educational and thoroughly enjoyable.

Antiquarian bookshops carry the finest in old and rare volumes. A scout might shop in one to find a book on the want list of a collector–customer.

Many antiquarian book dealers belong to a world-wide body devoted to fair practices in the buying and selling of old books. The name of this organization is the Antiquarian Booksellers' Association International. In the United States, it is known as the Antiquarian Booksellers' Association of America, Inc. (ABAA). If you want to know who the members are in your area, check the Yellow Pages of your phone directory under "Book Dealers." In some cities, ABAA members are listed under this category. For a full membership list of American members, send a request and self-addressed, stamped envelope to:

Antiquarian Booksellers' Association of America, Inc.
630 Fifth Avenue
New York, New York 10020

Membership in the ABAA has always been a good assurance that you will find a fair and honest dealer. In addition, it is a pretty good rule of thumb that any bookshop that has been in business for a while is probably honest. Book dealers who aren't honest don't usually last long. Book lovers and collectors can be clannish, and word gets around if a dealer overcharges or misrepresents the books in stock.

Antique Shops

Antique shops that carry a bit of everything may also stock a few old books. This is especially true of antique shops in areas where there are no old-book stores. Since many antique dealers are more interested in selling china, furniture, and old silver than they are in selling books, what few volumes they do have may be relegated to a box in a back room. So just because you don't see old books out front may not mean that a few volumes aren't tucked away somewhere. Always ask antique-shop proprietors if they have any books for sale.

There are, however, two reasons why it may not be good policy for a scout to buy books from an antique dealer. First, some old books in antique stores aren't actually there to be sold. Some shops use books to enhance their furniture. If you ask to buy such books, you may find that they have been priced deliberately high to discourage their sale.

The second reason you may not want to buy books from an antique store is that they may be poorly cared for. It is a shame to have to say this, but antique dealers will often take a great deal of time to restore and care for the furniture they have and neglect their antique books. If you are going to buy books in antique shops, take special care to check the condition of these volumes before you buy.

If you don't find the books you are looking for on the first trip, ask proprietors to call you when they return from buying trips and have books to sell. Leave your business card, and make a note in your files to call shop owners from time to time, or go to see if any books have come in.

Decorator Shops

Decorator shops are a second place scouts would do well to approach with caution. Like antique dealers, many interior designers buy books for display purposes only and mark them up to keep them from selling. Here, again, decorators may not be as careful about the care and restoration of their volumes as book dealers are.

One terrible example of this occurred when a large San Francisco department store had a carload of beautiful old books shipped from France for use in decorating the furniture department. Every book was given a heavy coat of shellac to make it look shiny, and then the books were placed on display and labeled as a "decorator item," which was all they could really claim to be. By the time the shellac was dry, the books were glued into solid blocks and were completely unreadable.

However, some decorator shops do have a few lovely old books for sale, so don't pass them by if you are searching for a special volume.

Book Fairs and Book Shows

Some of the best places to see fine books, learn about prices, and meet collectors who are interested in buying are book fairs and book shows. Some of these events are sponsored by chapters of the Antiquarian Booksellers' Association; some are sponsored by local libraries, schools, or collectors' clubs. At some shows, dealers pay a fee and take floor space for a sales booth. Scouts who are dealing in modestly priced books will not want to take a booth at a book fair, but attendance is well worth the price of admission. At fairs, you can learn a lot about pricing and what new collecting fads are developing, and you'll see, first hand, different types of rare books. Go to fairs early, and stay late; take along plenty of your business cards to distribute to prospective customers who will be milling through the aisles. Some book fair visitors are there just hoping to meet scouts selling moderately priced books.

Auctions

There are two different types of auctions a book scout may be interested in attending—those held in auction houses, and country auctions.

You will find the first place, the auction house or gallery, in large cities. Some cities have special auction galleries where only books are sold. These establishments put out catalogues and sales lists well in advance of auctions. Just by reading this material, you can learn a lot about how fine old books are described and priced. You can learn ten times more by going to an auction in person.

Beginning book scouts should learn to keep a tight grip on their purse strings when attending their first few auctions. There is always the risk of getting carried away by bidding fever and finding you have to take out a loan to pay for what you've bought. When you are learning about auctions, listen carefully, and keep your hands quietly in your lap. This last bit of advice is given for good reason. Some bidders make an offer merely by scratching an ear or adjusting their glasses.

If you should find a book that you have been trying to locate for a special customer listed in an auction catalogue, by all means try to buy it. If you aren't experienced enough to bid for it yourself, you can hire a dealer to do it for you. Some people make a business of executing bids for people they represent. The commission for this service starts at 10 percent of the book price. Be sure you tell your bidder what your top price will be, and be sure you have a firm buyer before you invest the money.

The second type of auction, the country auction, is quite common in many rural areas of the United States. The country auction may be held in a barn or barnyard, and the sale may include everything from a butter churn to a milk cow. If a whole estate is being auctioned off, you may be able to buy any books included from the bidder who gets the household goods. You may have to buy all of them. When you buy books by lot, be sure you don't let one or two good volumes convince you that the whole lot is worth buying. You can expect to get some junk, but don't buy a lot unless at least 75 percent of the books are resalable for a profit.

Collectors

Although collectors are always buying books, they are usually selling off a few volumes, too. Almost all collectors know what their books are worth, so you aren't likely to find great bargains; but since most collectors know how to care for books, you will probably find their sale items in good condition.

Collectors sell their books for a number of reasons; here are just a few:

- √ To eliminate duplicates. Many collectors can't resist buying a second copy of a book that is in better condition than the one they already own.
- √ To eliminate unwanted books acquired in lots.
- √ To weed out books that no longer interest them. Some collectors begin by accumulating all sorts of books and later concentrate on one type. Sale of early purchases can enable collectors to buy more books of the type they now collect exclusively.

Many collectors sell to other collectors. There is always a lot of trading back and forth between book lovers whenever they gather; and if you happen to be in the right place, with the right price, at the right time, your good offers are not likely to be turned down.

Here are some ways you can contact collectors about books they have for sale:

- √ Read book trade periodicals. A collector in your area may be advertising books for sale.
- √ Visit collectors' clubs. Nearly every city of any size has one or two of these clubs. If you are not permitted to visit meetings, write a letter to the chairman, and send a few of your business cards for distribution.
- √ Inquire at your local library. Many librarians are collectors or know others who are.

√Advertise. (See Chapter 6 for instructions on how to write an advertisement and what to include in it.)

Talk About Books to Everyone

Everywhere you go, talk to people about books—not just dealers and collectors, but everyone you meet. Ask people if they have books they want to sell. Tell them about the kinds of books you are interested in, and offer to come and see what they have tucked away that is no longer wanted. Some people never hold garage sales or give books to charity bazaars or thrift shops. These are just the individuals who might have a carton of resalable old volumes stored in a closet—volumes they might sell to you.

Look in the Telephone-Directory Yellow Pages

Whenever you travel to new areas, you will probably want to look over the junkshops, secondhand stores, and old-book stores you haven't explored before. There is always hope in the heart of a book scout that these green fields will produce something resalable. To save time, when you don't know the area, it is best to look in the Yellow Pages of a local telephone directory to locate old-book sources.

Look under these headings:

√*Book Dealers* (includes new, used, and antiquarian dealers)
√*Secondhand Dealers*

√*Thrift Shops*
√*Antique Dealers*
√*Book Auction Galleries*

A few minutes' research among the Yellow Pages before you actually go out will save you time and tired feet. You may want to call the places listed to ask about stock, business hours, and directions to the shop.

This final word about book search came from a wise old gentleman who had been a book scout for more than fifty years:

> Don't go to the big book shops in the big cities to look for old books if you hope to find bargains. Go out to the small towns and backcountry lanes. Ask people if they have books in their attics and barns they want to sell. Never wait until a book gets to market to buy it. Every time a volume changes hands, it becomes more expensive, and your profits are less. Don't wait for books to come to you. You go where the books are.

Secrets of Successful Book Buying

I F TWO BOOKS BY THE SAME AUTHOR, of the same edition, are for sale and one—in good condition— is priced at twenty dollars and the other—in poor condition—is priced at ten dollars, which book should you buy to resell?

If you chose the ten-dollar book in poor condition, thinking that you would save ten dollars, you made a serious error. You would not have saved ten dollars; you would have wasted ten dollars. A book in poor condition is not a bargain at any price, because it is not apt to resell.

THE CARDINAL RULE
FOR BUYING OLD BOOKS

In the real estate business, successful dealers live by this rule:

> When buying property for resale, the three most important qualifications to consider are—location, location, location.

This same principle applied to buying old books might be altered to read:

> When buying old books for resale, the three most important qualifications to consider are—condition, condition, condition.

If you buy books to resell for a profit, they must be in good condition. Do not buy a book in poor condition with an eye to restoring it, particularly if part of it has been destroyed. A torn HINGE, a HEADCAP that is worn away, a leather cover that is badly scuffed can never be completely repaired. You cannot replace what has been lost. Repairs of any kind do not enhance a book; they merely preserve it.

Likewise, books with missing PLATES, pages heavily underlined or stained, or ENDPAPERS that are torn cannot be brought back to fine condition. When you invest in a volume that you hope to resell, condition is an all-important factor.

Check the books you buy in person carefully. If you buy by mail, learn the vocabulary used in catalogues

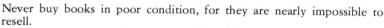

Never buy books in poor condition, for they are nearly impossible to resell.

and periodicals to describe book condition. These terms in descending scale are:

- ✓ Mint
- ✓ Fine
- ✓ Very good
- ✓ Good
- ✓ Fair
- ✓ Poor

See the glossary included in Chapter 9 for a full interpretation of these terms.

HOW TO JUDGE BOOK CONDITION

Since condition is such an important factor in deciding whether a book is resalable or not, knowing how to judge different elements of condition is vital to a book scout.

A book's cover is the first part a customer sees, and its beauty and condition may have a great deal to do with whether the book appeals to the customer, but there are many other parts of the book that should be checked out before buying. For example, no one wants to buy even a twenty-five-cent paperback novel if the last two pages are missing. And we've all admired lovely old children's books, only to open them and find crayon marks on the endpapers. A book with this kind of damage just won't sell.

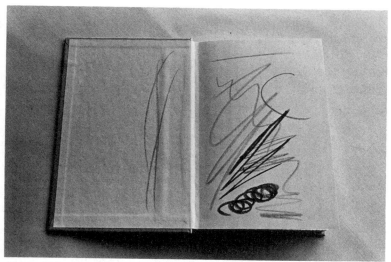
Never judge a book by the cover alone. Always look inside for defacing or damage.

No, you can't judge a book's resalability by its cover; there are so many other factors involved in judging overall condition. A condition checklist to go through before buying any book follows.

Cover

Part of a book's value depends on how it is bound. The skill of the binder and the material the binding is made of are both important. No matter how cheap a binding is, it should be strong enough to keep the book together so that the leaves do not come out. Today, books are bound in a wide variety of materials.

Modern pocketbooks have a paper binding and take their name, *paperbacks,* from this binding. Most of these books are considered throwaways, although some have a surprisingly long life.

Book club editions are often covered with cloth or synthetic leather. Both materials lend themselves to bright colors. Synthetic bindings, though certainly not valuable, are extremely durable.

Leather bound volumes in good condition are on the want list of almost every dealer. Learn to recognize the different types of leather bindings. Some kinds are much more valuable than others. Three of the most valuable leather bindings are as follows:

√*Vellum.* A fine white or cream-colored parchment prepared of untanned calfskin, lambskin, or kidskin.

√*Morocco.* A soft leather first made in Morocco of goatskin tanned with the powdered leaves of the sumac tree. It is now widely imitated.

√*Fur.* The dressed pelt of an animal. Pony or calf is the most often used fur, although books have been bound in the pelts of many exotic, short-haired animals. Very early tales of stag hunting were bound in the pelt of a stag.

The leather most commonly used for binding is calfskin, which can be dyed, stamped, and tooled rather easily. Calf is also used in making suede books. Suede is nothing more than a tanned leather with the flesh side out, buffed into a nap.

No matter how elegant a cover's material is, if that

cover is badly damaged, the book is not a good buy. Cover damage is pretty obvious as a rule and should take very little time to examine. It is not wise to buy books with covers that have:

√Tears, gouges, or scuffs

√Heavy stains

√Badly torn headcaps

√Cracked or torn hinges

√Shaken or loose bindings

√Heavily worn corners and edges

√Leather that is dry and flaking or that has red rot

√Heavy taping or gluing

√Lacquer or shellac

√Warping

End Papers

The type of paper used for end papers, that double leaf at the beginning and end of a book, and the condition of this paper help to determine a book's value. In rare, old, leather-bound books, the end papers are sometimes hand painted.

One method of making hand-painted end papers was to float oil paint of several colors on the surface of a large pan of gum solution and lower a sheet of paper dampened with alum water onto the paint. Paint that adhered to the paper was left to dry. Printers later copied these handmade designs, and today almost all end papers are mass printed.

Damaged or missing end papers can greatly detract from the beauty and value of a book. Some types of end-paper damage are as follows:

√*Missing end papers.* It is usually the front end paper that is most often missing. This is probably because the former owners wished to remove their bookplates or written name from the book before selling it. Sometimes, hand-painted end paper is removed to be sold separately.

√*Marred end papers.* End papers that have been written on or have had something pasted to them and torn out cause the book to be devalued, unless, of course, the writing is a famous signature.

√*Heavily stained end papers.* When a book is not wrapped during extensive cleaning or dyeing, the end papers can become stained at both back and front.

Always open a book at both the back and the front to check the condition of the end papers. Don't buy books with badly damaged end papers.

Illustrations

A book's value can be greatly increased by the number and quality of its illustrations. This fact is true of books ranging all the way from hand-illuminated manuscripts to modern photography volumes.

The earliest type of printed illustrations were wood engravings, made when images were cut in relief from blocks of wood. Wood engravings were followed by cut or etched metal plates that took on much more detail and were finer in line. Both methods are now widely imitated with modern reproduction techniques.

Before buying an illustrated book, always check the artwork for condition as well as quality. To assure that you are getting a resalable book, check the illustrations against this list:

✓*Are plates missing?* One of the most common kinds of damage in lovely, old illustrated books is the removal of valuable plates. Some book dealers sell valuable plates for framing and then try to sell the damaged book. Always check the list of illustrations against the remaining plates, to make certain the set is intact.

✓*Are plates free of amateur artwork?* Some people can't resist adding daubs of color to black-and-white books. This amateur artwork ranges all the way from childish crayon marks to faint water colors. None of these additions add to the value of the book unless the edition was commissioned that way.

✓*Are illustrations defaced?* Billboard portraits aren't the only ones to have mustaches drawn on them. Some people even draw cartoons in fine books.

✓*Is the register poor?* Bad printing, where a photograph or print is out of register, spoils an illustration.

✓*Are pages offset?* Fresh printer's ink may smear the

page opposite an illustration. Tissues are frequently inserted over each plate to prevent this defect.

√*Are plates torn?* Even small tears devalue a book.

√*Are plates stained?* Water or any other type of stain touching an illustration devalues the volume.

√*Is paper foxed?* Sometimes sheets of tissue covering an illustrated plate may be of different quality from those used for text and may be more heavily foxed. Check both text and plates for this defect.

Paper

Until the middle of the nineteenth century, paper was made almost entirely from rags, either linen or cotton. Pure rag paper is soft, slightly translucent, and lightweight. Early paper was laid down by hand and was often uneven and sometimes slightly lumpy in appearance. Modern paper is composed of any number of fibrous materials and is mass-produced on machines.

In bargain bookshops and secondhand stores, you aren't likely to find much in the way of handmade sheets of pure rag paper; but you should look for—and hope to find—soft, clean book paper of uncoated stock. Paper that is coated with a shiny surface is more apt to stick together if it becomes wet. Good, clean, soft paper is always more readable and adds to the value of a book.

Check for the following kinds of paper damage:

√*Water stains.* If a book becomes too wet, the fibers used to make the paper may start to disintegrate.

√*Mildew.* A book left in a damp, warm place may have spots and discoloration left by mold and will often have a strong, objectionable odor.

√*Foxing.* Pages stained a reddish-brown are said to be foxed.

√*Dog-eared corners.* The first person who thought of turning down the corner of a page to mark a place did a great disservice to the world of books. A corner turned down too often will eventually tear off.

√*Underlining.* Books with passages underlined or marked with read-through color pens are virtually unsalable.

Even this attractive miniature suede book is unlikely to resell, because it has been heavily underlined.

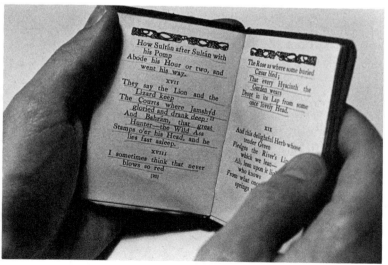

√*Margin notes.* A few light marginal notes made in pencil may be erased, but anything in ink or more extensive notations make the book unsalable.

√*Heavy or frequent stains.* People who eat while reading and allow grease and crumbs to stain the pages devalue the book. Some pages may even be marked with coffee-cup rings that go through several sheets.

√*Infestation.* More than seventy varieties of insects have been identified as enemies of books. These small creatures will devour cloth, leather, glue, and paper, making tunnels through pages and boards. Look closely at a clean page for spots, wormholes, dead or live vermin. One infested book can contaminate others; so no wise buyer is apt to want a book that shows signs of active infestation, and neither should you.

See Chapter 5 for a way to rid books of infestation.

Printing

Although it is acceptable for very old, hand-printed manuscripts to be faded and difficult to read, a modern book with indistinct printing is unsatisfactory. Books that are printed in pale ink, or on dark paper, or that use ornate and hard-to-read type usually are not good investments for resale. A scout should look for books with text that is clearly printed, unsmeared, and otherwise quite legible.

Bookmarker Ribbons

Many old books, and even some new ones, have silk ribbon bookmarkers that are fastened to the top of the book between the HEADBAND and the BACKSTRIP. Bibles sometimes have two ribbons to mark both the Epistle and the Gospel lessons.

Since many of these ribbons are very fragile, they often become frayed or torn off short. This loss detracts from a book's appearance, but new ribbons can be inserted; and if care is taken to use the same-quality ribbon as the original, the book will lose little value.

All types of heavy bookmarks should be avoided or removed, as they are apt to damage a book. Pressed flowers stain pages, clip-on bookmarks crease pages, and bulky enclosures put a strain on the book's binding and leave pages open to dust. Newspaper clippings left between pages will eventually stain the book paper. Newsprint, which is very cheap paper and highly acid, will eventually yellow and stain book paper.

Edges

How a book's edges are finished greatly affects its value. How the pages are separated after printing also affects resale price potential. Many types of modern books, such as textbooks and pocketbooks, have straight edges. These are made either by a guillotine blade or the cutting wheel on a web offset press. Cut edges are quite frequently sprayed with bright color.

Several types of fancy edges that add to a book's value are:

√*Feathered edge.* Made by pulling the paper over the sharp prongs of a steel comblike instrument to feather-cut the edge.

√*Deckle edge.* This edge is formed when the pulp flows against the deckle (pulp frame) on a sheet of handmade paper. The deckle edge is left untrimmed.

√*Gauffered edge.* When the cut edges of a book have a design pressed into them with a hot iron, the edges are said to be gauffered.

√*Hand-opened edge.* The fore-edge, and sometimes even the top and bottom edges, of a book may be creased and opened with a letter opener by hand.

√*Fore-edge painting.* The fore-edge is illustrated with a hand painting.

√*Tabulated.* Found most frequently in Bibles and reference books. The fore-edge is cut to accommodate tabs. In reference books, such as dictionaries, the tabbing is alphabetical.

√*Gilt-edge.* Said of a book whose page edges are gilded.

√*Quilled or marbled edges.* Said of a book that has edges of quilled or marbled design the same as end paper designs.

The edges of a book should be clean of spots, without writing or other identification marks. Look for library stamps on page edges, because these marks lower a book's value.

Dust Jacket

The first dust jackets, or DUST WRAPPERS, were nothing more than plain protective covers for decorative bindings. Today, dust jackets often carry eye-catching illustrations, a blurb (usually a high-caliber sales pitch), and a price. Many early dust jackets are now collectors' items. If a book still has its original dust jacket without tears, stains, tape, or fading, the book's value may be much higher. But even a fancy jacket won't help sell yesterday's book club edition or a volume in bad condition hiding under a crisp cover. In other words, don't judge a book by its dust jacket. Value must be in the book, or the combination of book and jacket will not be a good buy for resale.

Slip Case

Most cases, made for the protection of gift editions, are of pasteboard. Some cases are covered with hand-painted paper, and some are made of leather and lined with silk to protect very valuable books. Valuable miniature books are sometimes placed in gold or silver cases.

Books that have been kept in a slip case are usually in better condition than those without one. Cases offer support and prevent rubbing when being pulled off the shelf or when being pressed against other books. A full case prevents the binding from getting faded and keeps a book free of dust.

Look for two types of damage on books kept in open-ended cases:

√*Torn headcaps.* A book that is pulled from a case by the headcap rather than being tipped out can get torn.

√*Creased pages.* If care is not taken to assure that a book is completely closed before putting it into a case, pages jammed against the edge of the case will be creased.

A case may help sell a book, but again, a book should not be judged by its case. The resale value must be in the book itself.

Sets

Many collections of an author's complete works or long pieces of work are printed in several volumes or sets. Sets are usually identically bound and consecutively numbered. Many collectors and dealers will not buy partial sets. A part of a set—four volumes of a five-volume set, for example—has lost a large measure of its resale value. Before buying any set, make certain that all volumes are included and that all are in good condition.

Rebound Books

Although it is sometimes necessary to rebind a valuable old book to save it from falling apart and being lost in bits and pieces, restoration experts agree that whenever possible, it is best to try to preserve the original binding.

A good rebinding job should be consonant with the age and original style of the book, and a really fine rebinding is sometimes hard to detect. A book that has been rebound may have the bindery name noted in the upper left-hand corner of the inside of the FLYLEAF. Some, but not all, dealers will note rebinding in their catalogues.

Be cautious about investing money in fine editions that have been rebound. Many collectors buy only books in their original bindings. Never consider buying a book in poor condition to have it rebound.

A CHECKLIST FOR DETERMINING RESALABILITY

When you have found a book, checked it out, determined that it is in good condition, and are considering buying it for resale, ask yourself these questions before putting down your money:

1. Is the book priced low enough so that I can resell it at a profit?

2. What is the basic demand for the book? Does it have one of the following factors in its favor?
   √Is the book rare?

   √Is the book beautiful? (Remember, beauty can take many forms.)

   √Is the book in current demand for some reason?

√Has the book's subject or author stood the test of time?

But when all is said and done, a great deal of success in buying depends upon your eye and a feeling for what will sell—two things that come mainly with time and experience.

Home Remedies
for Book Care
and Repair

N INE OUT OF TEN BOOK SCOUTS say they never take any time to clean or make minor repairs to the volumes they buy for resale; yet just a short time spent cleaning a book can pay off in increased salability. Scouts who have the time should look over what they have purchased and give books the care they need to face resale in sparkling condition.

Many of the volumes you pick up for bargain prices in thrift shops and garage sales may be in basically good condition but a sad sight under a heavy coating of dust and grime. A few minutes' work with a clean cloth and a few rubs with a pink eraser can often change a book's entire appearance.

When you invest time and money in a book, taking a few more minutes to clean its cover and pages is a wise follow-up on that investment.

Since books are our friends, why not treat them that way? A bit of gentle care can bring out a book's true personality and beauty. Here are a few minimum-care suggestions that will pay off in increased salability.

DUST BOOKS

All books, regardless of age or type of binding, need dusting from time to time, but most volumes you are apt to pick up in bargain bins won't have been dusted well in a long time.

The most valuable suggestion that can be made in regard to dusting books is this: get rid of the dust—don't distribute it. Don't dust books by puffing and blowing the dust off bindings or by swishing over the top edges with a flapping cloth. This haphazard procedure only spreads the dust around.

Here is the correct way to dust a book thoroughly:

√Dust books one at a time.

√Hold the covers together tightly so the dust won't get between the pages.

√With a clean, soft cloth, wipe the top edge of the book from the spine to the fore-edge. Turn the cloth, and dust the remainder of the book. Change to a clean cloth every few books.

√Suede books should be dusted with a small, clean brush. Using light, even strokes, brush *with* the nap. Take care not to brush away any gilt lettering or designs.

Never dust furniture and books with the same cloth. Furniture oils will soil clean book edges.

REMOVE PENCIL
MARKS FROM PAGES

Secondhand book dealers think nothing of noting the price of a book in pencil on the end papers. If the writing has not made a deep indentation, these markings can be removed. Other light pencil marks that deface a book should also be removed.

A soft, pink eraser is the best kind to use on book pages. The Pink Pearl, found among the school supplies in dime stores, is a very good pink eraser. Make certain the eraser is clean before using it by rubbing old lead marks from it onto a sheet of unsoiled paper. Erase out from the center of the book to avoid wrinkling the pages. Avoid erasing on top of type, which can deface the print by smearing and fading it. When you have finished a page, dust out all eraser crumbs before going on to the next one.

Never buy a book that has marks made with a very hard lead pencil. Even when lead marking has been erased, the indentations will remain and deface the book.

MEND SMALL IMPERFECTIONS

A small bit of paste applied to the right place at the right time can diminish scars and tighten pages. Small tabs of leather that have come loose can be pasted down, and the flaw will become almost invisible. Loose leaves can be TIPPED IN with a bit of paste to keep them from being lost. The kind of paste you use for book mending is very important. Plastic adhesives oxidize, deteriorate, and discolor. Always use natural adhesives on books. The rule of thumb for book paste is: If you can't eat it, don't use it.

The best kind of paste for books is one you can make yourself in a few minutes using flour and water. Here is the recipe:

Flour Paste

Measure 1/2 cup refined, white flour into a saucepan.

Add 3/4 cup cold water, and stir the two together until mixture is smooth.

Cook the mixture over a slow heat, stirring constantly, until the liquid thickens and becomes a translucent paste.

Remove paste from heat, allow it to cool, and put it in a glass container with a tight lid. A clean, empty jam or pickle jar will do very nicely.

Store paste in the jar in the refrigerator when not in use. Make sure the lid is on tight. Paste will keep for several weeks.

After mending a book, always clean excess paste from any mended area, and put the book aside to dry completely before handling it again.

INCREASE THE LUSTER OF LEATHER BINDINGS

If you are lucky enough to scout out real leather bindings during your book search, you might want to spend a little time restoring the leather's luster. This slight effort will certainly increase the book's beauty— probably enough for you to raise its price a bit.

To lubricate leather bindings, use a solution of 60 percent neat's-foot-oil and 40 percent lanolin. This mixture can be made at home by combining both ingredients in the top of a double boiler and heating them slowly until blended. Neat's-foot-oil is sold in many hardware stores and saddlery shops. Lanolin is sold in most drugstores.

Here is the correct way to lubricate a leather book:

√ Wrap the pages in clean paper to prevent staining them.

√ Using a soft cloth or a ball of cotton, work the dressing into the leather. Special attention should be given to the spine, headcap, edges, and joints, for they may be especially dry.

√ Set the book aside to let the dressing be absorbed.

√ Using a clean dry cloth, wipe off excess dressing, and gently polish leather to a soft luster.

RID BOOKS OF INFESTATION

Before buying any book, look for bugs and worms or the holes, shredded paper, and excrement they leave behind. If you should be unlucky enough to have unwittingly purchased a book that is infested, isolate it from others to prevent the spread of this infestation. When any bugs, worms, or live larvae are detected, the book should be treated. Clean traces of infestation out from between all pages with a rag or soft brush. Next, the book should be rid of active infestation in the following manner:

√ Tie a bunch of freshly dried thyme into a porous cloth sachet. If you have thyme growing in your garden, this will be the strongest, but you may also use commercially tinned thyme. Never sprinkle thyme directly on the book, as it is apt to discolor the pages and binding.

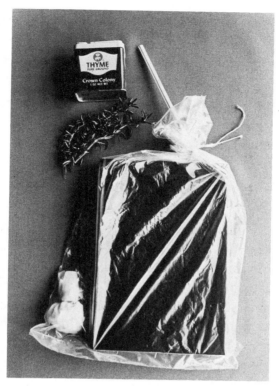

Seal a book in a plastic bag with a sachet of thyme
in order to free the pages of infestation.

√Place the sachet and the book in a plastic sack. The
kind of sack used for fresh vegetables in grocery
stores is excellent.

√Gather the sack together at the top, and place a
plastic drinking straw into the neck of the sack.

√Suck the air out of the sack with the straw, and tie
the gathered top shut with a string. You may leave

the straw tied in tightly or pull it out. Leave no air passage.

√Leave the book and thyme in the sealed sack in a warm place for two weeks.

√Isolate the book from others for two more weeks after removing it from the sack to make certain that all pages are free of infestation.

PROTECT BOOKS AGAINST ENEMIES

Books have many enemies, but one of the greatest is people, who soil, crease, tear, and write in books. They use books to sit on, stand on, place wet drinking glasses on, and even for propping open windows. Other book enemies are sun, fire, heat, water, insects, and decay. With so many enemies, it is a wonder that any really old books have survived at all.

For every enemy, however, there is a protective measure. Learn these simple safeguards to keep your books in top condition while they are in your possession.

Protect books against heat and strong sunlight.

√Store books away from heat vents, stoves, and fireplaces.

√Never put books near a window, a skylight, or anywhere they will be in the path of strong sunlight.

√Try to keep your book storeroom no warmer than sixty-five degrees.

Protect books against fire.

√Use good, household precautionary measures against fire.

Protect books against water and dampness.

√Do not store books in humid areas such as basements or garages.

√Do not store books under water pipes or near water heaters.

√If you store books in an attic, make certain the roof does not leak.

Protect books against infestation.

√Quarantine all newly purchased books until they have been found free of infestation.

Protect books against theft.

√While you are away from a vehicle, keep books out of sight by locking them in the car trunk.

Protect books from excess handling.

√Hand customers books one at a time when showing them. Wait until a person has finished looking at a book, take it back, and then hand him or her another. This way, you will prevent your books from being dropped or put down carelessly.

√Whenever possible, show books to customers by placing them flat on a table. Several can be seen at one time this way without risk of being dropped.

Prevent books from being dropped by displaying them on a table or by handing them to a customer one at a time.

√If you have fore-edge books, always show them yourself, holding them by the top and bottom edges of the pages to flex them without putting your fingers on the painting. Draw the book back slightly if customers try to touch the painting.

√Show miniature books only to interested customers. Since miniatures have so little weight, they are apt to fan open or YAWN if they are frequently opened.

PROTECT BOOKS WITH
SPECIAL STORAGE
PROBLEMS

Most of your books won't be storage problems, since it is hoped that they will not be in your possession for long. The longer a book sits unsold, the more profit is eaten up. However, there are some types of books that need special care when stored for any amount of time.

The following books have special shelf problems:

Very Large Books

If large books are stacked more than three or four deep, their great weight can cause newly printed text to offset, one page on another. And when oversized books are pulled from a shelf, they wear badly on the bottom edge because of their weight. Store FOLIO-SIZE books on their side with only a few books to a stack.

It is also wise when opening and closing very large books to make certain that the end papers and the first few pages are lying flat between the covers. Large sheets tend to fall toward the GUTTER and crease if this precaution is not taken.

Suede Books

The bottom of the soft binding of a suede book can become crushed or even torn when the book is stored on end. Suede books are best stored lying flat.

Suede books should not be kept on a shelf on end, because their soft bindings are apt to become crushed. Suede books are best stored lying flat.

Vellum Books

Support VELLUM books with bookends, and be especially careful to keep them dry, but not in very warm areas, since vellum—which is untanned leather—is especially susceptible to changes in humidity. This is why you see so many warped vellum books.

Books with Bosses

BOSSES, the metal knobs meant for the protection of a leather binding, can cause damage to books stored next to them. Always place firm pasteboard dividers between books with bosses and other volumes. Protect furniture from being scratched by placing such books on a cloth to show them.

PROTECT BOOKS THAT MUST BE PUT AWAY

If it is necessary for some reason to store your books for any period of time, each book should be placed in an individual plastic sack and sealed. Suck the air out of the sack with a straw before tying the top shut. Books enclosed in this manner are protected against dampness, infestation, and mold for long periods of time.

Put Up a Fence

People protect most things of beauty and value. Fences are put around gardens to keep out stray pets. Delicate objects of art are kept behind glass. Jewels are displayed on pads of velvet. Flowers, silver, jewels, even automobiles are protected, but often fine libraries of beautiful old books are left uncared for.

Even books in mint condition need care to prevent their deterioration. Beautifully made books need more than admiration. Books can't just be put on a shelf and left for years without some kind of regular care. They need to be cleaned and fed, checked for infestation and mold, and protected against their enemies. When you invest time looking for books and the money to buy them, you should protect this investment. Book care is just another way of putting a fence around something you value.

6

How to Find
Book Customers

FINDING SALABLE BOOKS at reasonable prices is only half of a book scout's job. Finding interested buyers and selling books to them are necessary if you are going to keep the wolf from the door.

Just finding a book that is priced below the value given in some catalogue doesn't mean a sure sale. Buyers aren't going to be waiting at your door ready to hand you money. You're going to have to go out and find customers. Few books sell themselves, and if you are going to be a professional book scout, the sooner you realize this fact, the sooner you'll begin to make a profit. Professional scouts make the effort to seek out the customers who are likely to offer the best price for any book they have to sell. Never be satisfied with selling to just any customer when, with a little more effort, you can find one who will pay you more.

It may be easy to pick up a few nice books at a bazaar and sell them for a small but quick profit to the little secondhand bookshop down the street, but it's not good business. Good, professional book scouts make the effort to check out several outlets. Even if some turn them down, they continue to hunt for a customer who really wants the book they have for sale and will offer the top price.

Some buyers are always willing to pay more for the books they want. Finding that type of buyer is what success is all about. Whether you deal in rare books, comic books, or secondhand-store bargains, this rule applies.

Because prices for old books are unstandardized, no two selling days will ever be alike. Prices reflect special interests, local interests, and subject areas in current demand. Specialized interests vary from day to day, pulling prices with them. However, certain types of customers will always pay a better price than others.

On the next few pages, different types of buyers and book outlets are listed with instructions on how to locate them. The best-paying markets are listed first. The list works on down to the markets that won't even offer you a break-even price; but they are important to know about, too, when it's time just to get some unwise buys off your hands.

TYPES OF CUSTOMERS

Private Collectors

If you have the kinds of books that are in collectible categories and in top condition, try to sell them to collectors first. Some avid collectors would willingly deprive themselves of any number of the necessities of life to gain a desired volume. Collectors read about books for sale, spend their spare time in bookshops, belong to book clubs, and attend auctions and book fairs. Collectors are the top market for your books, and if you become a reliable supplier of the types they want, they may even seek you out and tell other collectors of your services.

Auction Houses

If an auction house or gallery will accept your books to auction off on commission, you have a fine chance of selling them for a good price. It stands to reason that auction houses do not accept books they do not think they can sell, so acceptance for placement in a catalogue almost always means that you will find a bidder.

You have a right to set a reserve price on your books below which you refuse to go. If bidding does not come up to that price, your books will be returned to you. Most auction houses will not charge a commission on any books that are returned to you.

Many auction houses will buy books from scouts outright. This type of sale will give you a quick return on your investment, but you could very likely get a better price if you gambled on having those same books auctioned off and being paid a commission. Perhaps the deciding factor should be the date set for the auction, which will determine the length of time you would have to wait for the books to sell. If you are running on a very tight budget, you won't be able to afford much waiting time.

Book Customers (Not Collectors)

Some book lovers just like to accumulate vast numbers of books in no specific category. These people are not collectors, so they probably won't have specific want lists, but they are good paying customers.

Many book lovers also buy books as gifts. Fine bindings, suede books, miniatures, and picture books are popular gift items that will sell readily.

Noncollectors are not as particular about content or the particular edition of a certain book as collectors are, but many insist that books be in fine or near-mint condition.

Book Dealers

An amazing amount of bookselling goes on back and forth among dealers and scouts. This kind of exchange can be profitable for both. You may buy from dealers to get certain books you want for good customers, and you may also sell to dealers when they have a customer for a certain volume you have. Scouts also sell to one another.

The dealers who will pay the top price for your books are, of course, the *antiquarian book dealers*. If you happen to be lucky enough to find a book of the rarity and quality they are seeking, take it to them first.

Secondhand bookshops that handle very few rare books or collectible books but have a good trade in reading copies are very good book scout customers. Most shop owners have few employees and are too busy keeping their shops open to have much free time to scout books, so they welcome scouts who bring in resalable volumes. It is always wise to cultivate the friendship of one small shop owner who will buy your less expensive books.

HOW TO CONTACT CUSTOMERS

It is all very well to say that you should try to sell your books to collectors, but how to find those customers may be a technique you also have to learn about. Customers at all levels, but especially collectors, may seem well hidden until you learn how to contact them. Of course, you should always try first to contact the best-paying customer for the type of book you have. Here are a few suggestions for ways to contact different types of buyers:

How to Contact Collectors

Here are some of the best ways of getting in touch with collectors:

- √Ask your local librarian for names of collectors and collectors' clubs in your area.

- √Write local clubs, and ask permission to visit. Enclose several business cards in the letter. Even if you aren't given permission, your cards may be distributed to members, and you may make some contacts that way.

- √If you are allowed to visit a club meeting, take only your best volumes to show. Be organized about your sales presentation, and take up only a limited amount of club members' time.

- √If a club runs a newsletter, ask if you may buy some advertising space. Study book ads in other periodicals, and pattern yours after the best. Make your notice short and simple, and be sure to include your phone number. An address is fairly useless since most people do not want to take the time to write.

- √Take advertising space in local newspapers, book trade periodicals, or the telephone-book Yellow Pages. Again keep the concept of your ad simple.

√If your local supermarket has a community bulletin board, ask if you may post a notice offering books for sale and asking to buy old books. Type your notice in capital letters, and mat it on bright paper to make it stand out from the handwritten, recipe card notices. Again, use your phone number.

√Build a mailing list of collectors by keeping names and addresses of all former sales contacts, people you meet at clubs, auction houses, and book fairs. Send out a regular direct-mail letter to those on this list offering to buy and sell books.

Advertise by posting notices on community bulletin boards. This is a good way to find new customers at no cost.

How to Contact Auction Galleries

Look in the Yellow Pages under "Auction Galleries," and phone to find out those who handle old books. Go to the gallery nearest you in person, and take the books you have to sell. Know what price you want before going. Don't ask gallery owners to make you an offer. Auction houses aren't in the business of giving out free appraisals. If a gallery accepts your books, they will be auctioned, and a commission based on a percentage of the price received for them will be charged.

If your books are rejected, politely ask why. Maybe you have priced them wrong, or perhaps they are simply not salable. You learn about buying from the rejections you receive.

How to Contact Customers Who Are Not Collectors

Buyers who are not collectors but who accumulate books for themselves and for gifts congregate at many of the same places book collectors do. Here is a list of ways to contact these buyers:

1. Go to book fairs, book shows, and book exchanges. Give out your card, and ask those buyers who appear interested in scouting services to give you their addresses.

2. Have your own sale if you have enough books. It need be nothing more elaborate than a garage sale that offers only books. You will be amazed at the number of people who respond.

√Plan your sale well in advance, and advertise in your neighborhood shopping news.

√Post notices of the sale on community bulletin boards.

√Put out signs on street corners near your residence.

√Price your books fairly, and display them attractively on tables, where they can be seen, rather than in boxes.

√Hold out for your listed price. Don't allow a bidder to offer you a lesser price or a price for the entire lot. A good-paying buyer may be the last customer to walk into your garage.

How to Sell to Dealers

Establish yourself as a reliable and honest source of supply at one or two dealers. Try to find out just what kind of books these dealers are interested in, and look for that type when you are out on a book search.

If you should fail to sell a group of books to your regular dealers, take them to other stores in the area. Select the better stores, and go to them first; work down to the poorer-paying outlets later. When you get down to the level of junkshops who have only a few boxes of books, you may as well forget about selling for a profit. You may break even if you are lucky.

If All Sales Outlets
Turn You Down

If you have tried every outlet that you can think of and still can't sell your books, take them to a charity outlet and donate them. Ask for a receipt. Take a tax deduction for a business loss for the amount you originally paid for these books.

A *Lesson Learned from Loss*

The harder a time you have selling your books, the more you should think about and study the market before you buy again. Books that won't resell obviously weren't good buys when you acquired them. Don't buy that kind of book again unless the market changes radically. Continue to study the current book market at every opportunity. Don't let one or two defeats discourage you. Begin again with a new batch of books. Buying and selling are the best ways to learn how to upgrade your skills.

How to Sell Like an Expert

T HE BASIC RULES FOR SELLING BOOKS are much the same as those for selling any type of merchandise. Selling is not a matter of luck; it's a combination of hard work and experience.

Nearly every successful salesperson has these three basic qualities:

√*Personality.* Likes people and has a sincere desire to help them. Is self-confident and poised. (Shy and insecure persons can never make it as book scouts, who have to poke their noses into too many strange places in search of customers and books.)

√*Attitude.* Is enthusiastic about the work and the product offered for sale. (Book scouts have to love books, or the whole game just isn't worthwhile.)

√*Work Habits.* Sets goals, plans ahead, and keeps to a schedule. Is industrious and hard working. (Remember that the other name for book scout is *runner*.)

If the three-quality profile sounds like you, then you are probably going to make a good book salesperson. Sales are half the success of being a good book scout.

When book lovers start out to sell, they already have two factors in their favor. The fact that they love books means they will be selling a product they are enthusiastic about. And the fact that they personally selected the books they will sell means that they believe these volumes are resalable. However, a good product does not always mean a sure sale. Poor techniques can mean the loss of a sale. Even a small mistake like calling on a customer at the wrong time of day can mean rejection. To make successful sales, don't make obvious mistakes; heed the helpful steps that follow.

KNOW THE MARKET

Today's book market is dual in nature, because there are two types of buyers out there. One type still wants quality books to read and keep, as book lovers have always done. The other type wants cheap pocketbooks to read and throw away or recycle for more pocketbooks. These paperback readers are apt to buy a book during lunch hour, begin to read it on the commuter bus going home from work, decide they don't like the book, and toss it into the nearest trash can at the bus stop.

The first kind of buyer, the one who still buys hardbound books to keep, is the book scout customer. Unfortunately, people who are interested in accumulating a library are greatly outnumbered by the paperback readers. Fewer and fewer individuals are keeping books once they have read them, but there are two good reasons for this trend.

First of all, most modern homes are much smaller than those built for our parents. Today, only the homes of the very wealthy have rooms called libraries, and even built-in bookcases are nearly a thing of the past. With housing costs at so much per square foot, today's house must be usable as living space, not storage space for books.

The second reason more people aren't accumulating libraries is that so many families move about a great deal more than they once did. When every pound that goes into the moving van is weighed, books are one of the heavy items that are often left behind.

So today, great numbers of people never buy anything but paperback books, even if they intend to give them as gifts. If a book these buyers want comes out in hardcover, they simply wait until the paperback edition is issued before buying.

This change in the market is something you should thoroughly understand, because it is going to affect your sales as a book scout. Bookstores selling new and used paperbacks are now doing a thriving business. Even local libraries are partially stocking their shelves with paperbacks. Only special kinds of buyers are looking for hardcover books today, and only special kinds of shops are interested in stocking old hardbound volumes. You're going to have to look harder for customers than scouts did fifteen years ago, just as you are going to have to look harder for book bargains. But that doesn't mean there isn't still opportunity out there. Finding customers calls for a study of the market in depth, and that means knowing your local book market.

Begin your local market survey by finding out how many used book stores there are in your immediate area or within a ten-mile radius. Look in the telephone book Yellow Pages for this information. Visit the shops listed, and see what their buying interests are. Find out if they buy only paperbacks, only hardbacks, or both. If you live in an area where only a few shops are interested in buying anything hardbound, you may want to consider transporting your books to another market area if transportation costs are not prohibitive. If you have a car, load up your trunk with books, and make sales trips.

Another way to sell in your area, and within a radius even greater than ten miles, is to offer books by direct advertising or by direct-sales letter. You may turn up customers in the next block, where you thought there were none, using one of these methods.

Direct-Advertising Tips

Direct advertising is expensive, but it may turn out to be the most profitable way for you to sell. Write short, simple ads offering to buy and sell used books. Use your phone number for customer convenience.

Try advertising in the small, local papers first. Rates for space in a shopping newspaper are less than in a large paper. Of course, you won't have a large circulation to draw on, but start small to learn what ads attract the most customers. Any answers will also help you to build an address list for a direct-sales letter.

Direct-Sales-Letter Tips

Letters can bring very effective returns for the amount they cost if you are selective about your mailing list. Build your list slowly and carefully before you plan to send out a letter. Always keep candidates for a mailing list in mind when you visit collectors' clubs, book fairs, auctions, and other dealers. Set up a file with names of prospective customers, and when you are ready to send

Send prospective customers personal letters. Ask to buy the books they no longer want, and offer to find books on their want lists.

out a sales letter, your mailing list will already be established.

Next to using a selective mailing list, most important is that you word your letter well. The most effective one is individually typed on your business stationery. Format for a direct-sales letter should follow along these lines:

√In the first sentence, offer to help your readers by asking to buy the books they no longer want.

√Say you will pay the fair market price for any book you decide to purchase.

√Ask customers to call you. Give your phone number in the body of the letter as well as at the top of the stationery.

√Offer to help your readers find books they have on their want lists.

√Offer to send readers a list of books you have for sale.

Always follow up promptly on any answers you receive, either from direct advertising or your direct-sales letter. If your first mailing is unrewarding, go over your list again, but be very careful about eliminating names. Mail another letter in a few weeks. In this second letter, list books for sale. This time, you may get replies.

Don't be discouraged if you do not hear from ads and letters in the first few days. Both these contacts have remarkably long lives, especially the sales letters. You may receive a reply even months after you have written.

KNOW YOUR BUYER

Equally as important as knowing the market is knowing the buyers. Find out as much as possible about the people who are your prospective customers before you go out to sell to them. The more you know about customers, whether they be shop owners, collectors, or other book scouts, the more apt you are to make a sale.

Know what type of books your buyer wants, and offer that buyer only that type of book. For example, if you are trying to sell to a bookstore owner who specializes in religious books, don't bring that person books about baseball. You waste the customer's time and your own when you do this, and you lose some of your credibility with that buyer.

Know your buyer's price range. Don't bring $200 books to the collector on a $10 budget; again, you waste time.

Know when to call on your customer. Don't call on shop owners during their rush hours.

When buyers learn to depend on you as a reliable source of the type of books they want and can afford, they will gladly give you the time to call on them and show your product. This is true of every kind of buyer—from collector to junkshop dealer. All customers value their time, and you should, too. Know in advance how to please the buyer.

KNOW YOUR PRODUCT

Learn everything you can about the books you have to sell before you go out to sell them. If you have a box of old cookbooks, you may want to offer them all to one dealer, or you may want to take out one or two special volumes and sell these to a collector, thereby making a better profit. You can only determine this sales tactic by studying the product.

Generally, what you will want to emphasize in your sales pitch is a volume's best features. Examine the book to determine this. On a slip of paper, list the book's fine features and the price you have decided to ask. Place the slip of paper inside the book's cover. When you meet with your buyer, pull out the slip of paper, and mention each fine feature. For example, if a book has fine paper, a nice binding, electrotypes of original wood engravings, or is on a subject in demand, you should be aware of these features and mention them to the buyer. Don't lose money on a sale because you don't know what you have to offer. Look over each book when you buy it and again when you price it for resale.

Always mention all of a book's fine features *before* you give the asking price. Even if your customer asks prices right out, try to get your feature list mentioned before the price.

PRICE YOUR BOOKS FAIRLY

There are many variables in book pricing. You should be aware of all of them before you go out to sell books. The three most important factors influencing price are:

1. *When a book is sold.* The state of the economy, both local and national, has an influence on what you will be

able to ask. When money is scarce, even valuable old books sell for less.

A customer's personal budget also influences buying. Some people spend more freely right after payday. And even secondhand bookshops buy more stock before Christmas than they do in January before inventory.

2. *Where a book is sold.* A volume that is offered for sale where there is a surplus of the same type of book will not bring as great a price as if it were scarce.

Specialized books sell better when they are near the area of specialization. For example, books about Florida sell better in that state than they do in Vermont. And books about growing citrus fruit sell better in warm climates than they do in cold.

3. *What book is sold.* A pretty little suede volume of poetry may look like it is worth more than a beat up old history book; but the poetry may be unprofitable to handle, whereas the history, which just happens to be a rare edition, may bring a very good price. A book scout must continually study to be able to recognize what kinds of books are valuable.

There is no pat formula for arriving at a final price. Any good book scout will tell you that in order to make a profit, your markup for a book should be at least 50 percent over what you paid for the volume. Some scouts mark everything up 75 percent. However, if you price your books over the going market rate, you will lose your trade, so you must always price carefully if you intend to stay in business. And if *you* paid too much for a book, this does *not* mean that you can pass the error off on your customer by charging too much for its resale.

Pricing is the most difficult part of your job, but you must know what you want for a book before you go to a customer with it. No dealer or customer wants to price your books for you. It is the mark of an amateur not to have a price on a volume one is trying to sell. Many dealers simply will not buy from someone who does not set prices. Private buyers and collectors also expect you to know what you want for what you are offering. Many collectors know exactly what a book is worth, but they want you to tell them.

There is really no easy way to come up with a never-fail method of pricing books. What a book is worth varies with location and situation. You have to be in a location and know the market situation there when you price the book to determine its resale potential. You learn how to price from experience, and that experience includes making some mistakes and taking a loss on them.

Pricing experience can be learned in any or all of these ways:

√Work as an apprentice for a time in a used-book store.

√Buy and sell books, and learn by trial and error.

√Read catalogues and book trade periodicals.

√Go to auctions and book sales.

√Visit bookshops, and price the stock.

Finally, one day you will find yourself looking at a book and knowing what it is worth, how much you can resell it for, and who is likely to buy it. At that moment, you will have arrived as a successful book scout.

HOW TO MAKE A BUSINESSLIKE SALES PRESENTATION

The way you present your books, your demeanor, and your conduct during your sales proposal can make the difference between being turned down and making a sale. Much of your success will depend upon how well you prepare for your presentation in advance. Use the following checklist to make sure you are ready for customer contact.

√Dust your books, make minor repairs, and erase pencil marks.

√Price your books, and list that price and the book's outstanding features on a card; insert the card in the front of the book.

√Pack your books carefully in a small box or briefcase. The way you handle your books shows that you value them.

√Show only a limited number of books at one meeting. Don't overwhelm any buyer, collector, or dealer with a vast number of volumes all at once.

√Use time to your advantage. Try to sell your books during the hours the buyer will find convenient.

Call in advance for an appointment, and be on time.

√Keep to the business you have come to conduct. Be brief and businesslike in your presentation. Stay only as long as your customer wishes to look at your books.

√Strive for a neat and conservative appearance that will encourage confidence.

WHAT TO SAY TO MAKE A SALE

Smile when you approach your customer, and call that customer by name. Try to say something sincerely complimentary or pleasant. When you are showing books to a store owner, mention something you like about the store. When you are showing to private collectors, say something enthusiastic about their collection.

Be easy, friendly, and sincere, but don't waste your customer's time. After you have greeted your customer, get down to business—show what you have to sell.

Present your books with enthusiasm. Say something like this:

"I have some good books to show you today that I think you're going to like."

Never start with this type of negative comment:

"I don't know if these are the sort of books you buy, but I thought I'd bring them around anyway."

Whenever possible, hand books to customers one at a time, and allow them to look each one over carefully before you go on to the next. While a customer is looking at a book, mention its good features. Use the notes you wrote down and inserted with the price slip. Answer any questions fully whenever you can.

If your customer looks over a book quickly and rejects it before you've even had time to mention its good features, take time to mention them anyway. You may change his or her thinking.

Some dealers try to buy books for less than they are worth from inexperienced sellers. They often do this by making negative remarks about the volumes offered. For every negative remark you hear, try to have a positive reply in mind. Here are a few remarks you may hear from buyers and ways to counter them:

"Your price is too high."	Don't back down on price once you have worked out what you think you ought to charge. Tell the customer your price is based on the fair market value.
"This type of book isn't selling this year."	Certain types of books always sell well (art books, cookbooks, fine bindings). Override this objection with a positive comment about one of the book's good features.

"I don't think I can afford to buy anything right now."	Don't believe this. You were given an appointment to come and show your books, and if the customer didn't have any money, you wouldn't be there. Go over the book's good features again.
"I already have a copy of this."	If the copy you have for sale is in fine condition, ask if the customer's copy is as fine. Collectors are especially apt to buy a second copy to get one in better condition.

Ask for a sale. If you don't ask your customers to buy your books, you make it too easy for them not to. Always finish off your presentation with a request for a sale. You might say something like this:

"Shall I write up a sales slip for these?"
"I'll bet you want this beauty."
"Which books do you want today?"
"Would you like to buy the whole lot?"

When you put the words of sale into your customer's mind, you make it harder for him or her to refuse you.

WHEN AND HOW TO
ACCEPT REJECTION

If all your positive remarks do not bring an offer to buy, accept the fact that the buyer really means *no*. Lose gracefully and smile, even as a customer turns you down. Try not to show your disappointment in any way. Continue to be friendly, and say something positive like:

> "I think I now have a better idea what type of book you want. The next time, I'll bring a different type of selection, something more to your liking."

This kind of closing remark and a friendly tone allow you to leave with good feeling, and the prospect of your being allowed to come back another day is very good.

When your sales efforts are rejected (and every book scout is rejected from time to time), don't go home and sit around and brood about it. Brooding is a waste of good time. Instead of slowing down your activity, pick it up. Try the next customer on your list. That customer may want every book you offer. Remember, it takes persistence and courage to be a book scout, but if you have those attributes, you'll sell.

Offering your books on the market is the true test of your ability to buy well. The odd volumes of sets, the torn covers, the editions with missing pages that you thought were such bargains will be seen in their true light when you go out to sell them. Beginners learn this way.

BUILD YOUR BUSINESS

The best and most reliable source of business is repeat business. When your satisfied customers call you again for their book needs, you know you are on your way to success. And when you are recommended to other customers by word of mouth from these customers, that is the best advertising you can get.

Continue to strive to strengthen your relationships with present customers. Contact them regularly by phone and direct mail. Remember, you can only build your business one customer at a time, so give each customer a share of your time and attention. Keep want lists in mind, follow up on orders promptly, and don't let down on your standards even if you are rushed.

LEARN TO SET A PACE

One of the important lessons all book scouts need to learn is how to pace themselves. Books scouts are called *runners* because they run to find books, and they run to find customers, and then they run to find more books. But all running and no rest can soon mean a burned out book scout. The job calls for an everyday steady pace, but not a killing grind. It is true that contact with sources and customers should be constant or those contacts will sell books to someone else and those customers will buy from other scouts; but when you find yourself not loving books anymore because of the pressure of the job, that is the time to let up. If you should decide to give up being a book scout, you may lose more than just an occupation. You may become disenchanted with books, and then you will have lost a lifetime love and interest. So pace yourself; go at being a book scout as though it were a business—but not a drudgery.

There are several ways book scouts can pace themselves while still carrying on a good business. A few practical suggestions follow.

Specialize

Some scouts buy and sell only one type of book. This specialization often grows out of a collecting interest or particular knowledge. For example, if a scout already knows a great deal about children's books, art, oceanography, or some other field, then that field would be a natural for specialization. If you have a great interest in one particular subject, then focus on that subject. Certainly, it would make your job that much easier to work in a field you already know a lot about. There are other advantages in specializing, too. Here are some of them:

√Specialists become known by the type of books they handle and are sought out by dealers and collectors who have an interest in that field.

√Scouts can advertise in periodicals related to their field.

√Collectors' clubs sometimes keep lists of specialists to distribute to their members.

√Scouts who specialize in only one field can study

the technical aspects of that field in greater depth than those who have to relate to many areas.

Of course, there are disadvantages in specializing, too. Scouts who limit the type of book they sell also limit their market. And scouts who are specialists must look longer to find books in their field while passing up bargains in other fields.

Sell by Direct Mail

Some book scouts, especially those who do not like direct contact with customers, sell by direct mail. They advertise for want lists, answer want-list advertisements, and advertise books for sale. This kind of selling can sometimes be expensive. If ads do not bring answers, the money for the ad is wasted. And with higher postage, even book rates are costly, so mailing books can cut into profits. But for the scout who may find it difficult to meet customers in person or to travel about, selling by mail is ideal.

Add Another Line

If in your travels off looking for books, you come across other resalable items such as antique toys or cut glass, you may want to scout in more than one line. Adding another line may increase your profits without adding to your scouting trips, but it will increase your need to seek out customers as well. More than one line calls for contact with different types of dealers and collectors. However, some scouts find that dealing in more than one type of salable item adds to their interest in the job.

Become a Restoration Expert

Artisans who restore and repair fine books are greatly needed. Of course, this kind of work takes a long period of study and apprenticeship, but it is rewarding both monetarily and in satisfaction. And for those who do not want to go into fine binding, there is work to be done on the repair and rebinding of library volumes and family books of lesser value. For scouts who are tired of running, there is the field of book restoration if they are willing to learn the trade.

THERE'S ALWAYS WORK FOR BOOKWORMS

So if you love books, like being around them, like to read books, talk about books, and take care of books, there's certainly a lot of work to be done in the field. If scouting is too tough, or if restoration is not something you think you are talented enough to take on, there's still a wide world of bookstore work out there and a place for you to get involved with something you love.

Be Your Own Boss

THE FINE LINE between being a professional book scout and a well-meaning amateur may simply lie in the matter of attitude. Professionals approach book scouting as a business—not a hobby. This chapter offers some business tips on how beginners can become professionals in the book scouting field.

Having your own business, with the right to make all the decisions, can be a heady experience—especially when you first realize that all the profits from that business belong in your pocket. But sole control can be a scary experience as well, because all the bills, all the gripes, and full credit for all the mistakes are yours, too.

But if you've always wanted to have a try at being your own boss, managing a business of your own, being free to work exactly as you please, any time you please, you'll love being a book scout. If you like books and enjoy meeting people, you already have the two most important attributes needed for success in the scouting field.

BASIC RULES FOR BUILDING A SOLID BUSINESS

Professional book scouts set goals and follow through on them. In the process of doing this, they live by these rules:

1. *Be Willing to Learn.*

Even if you've been a book lover or collector for a large part of your life, changing your hobby into a business means you may have a lot to learn. Never close your mind to new facts and ideas. Don't skip over the technical aspects of running your business, or you may find yourself in a tax bind or heavily in debt.

You can learn a lot by watching other scouts. If you possibly can, try to watch a good book scout in action. You may even become an apprentice to one to get some good basic training. Watch techniques used by successful scouts when buying and selling. If you can get one of them to stand still and answer your questions, find out if they advertise and where. Note where they go to find bargains. Never be afraid to copy success.

Listen to book dealers, who may be your best customers if you learn what they want to buy.

Get to know as many collectors as you can. Attend collectors' meetings that are open to visitors.

Try to keep ahead of buying trends. Read want lists in book trade periodicals. Remember, new popularity trends are always emerging. Books that went begging, that nobody could sell yesterday, may be today's fad.

Study your customers constantly. The collector who has turned you away three times may buy on your fourth attempt because you finally learned what kind of book he or she wanted.

You can learn something each day from your working experiences. Your early mistakes and failures can lead to greater profits later on if you learn by them. If your first few purchases result in a loss, try to determine whether you bought the wrong kind of book or whether you paid too much for what you bought to make a profit at resale. A mistake or two at the beginning can be your certificate to later success if you analyze your actions to find out what you did wrong and if you learn not to make those mistakes again.

2. *Keep Your Contacts Current.*

People have short memories. If you don't keep offering your good customers a constant stream of collectible books, they will turn to other scouts. If you don't make the rounds of the places that supply you with books, those outlets will sell to others. Constantly strive to keep up your good contacts. If you can't always call on people in person, pick up the phone, and let them know you are still in business. A call means good will, and good will is one of your best sales tools.

3. *Turn Your Books Over Fast.*

Once you have purchased a book, sell it as soon as you can. Books sitting around in boxes mean that your money is tied up. Wealthy speculators may be able to hold on to books until they are worth many times what they paid for them, but book scouts—operating on a limited amount of cash—can't afford to tie up capital this way. Keep turning your stock over. Don't let books sit on a shelf and eat up your profits. If one outlet turns you down, immediately go to another, and sell for less if you must.

4. *Use Time and Money Wisely.*

A book scout's two most important resources are time and money. Even if you have a lot of both, don't waste either one.

Time wasted can mean a loss of profit. You can double or triple your profits by wise use of time. Never make a trip to visit one buyer when you can visit two or six on the same trip. Never call on one customer when you can go to a book club meeting in the same amount of time and talk with ten.

Saving time often goes hand in glove with saving money. When you double up on errands by visiting more than one customer or one source of supply, you make better use of your time and get double duty for your transportation dollar as well. Money is your second important resource. If you are a beginner, money may be even more limited than time. Constantly seek to manage your pennies wisely. Real professionals are concerned with cutting both large and small costs. Little expenses—like extra trips to the post office, waste of supplies, or the use of too much postage—can add up to a big loss.

Here is a list of practical money-saving suggestions that every business professional who wants to cut down on costs would do well to follow:

√If a letter will do the work, don't make a long-distance phone call.

√Pick up the phone, and make local calls to save the time needed to write a letter and the postage it would cost to mail that letter.

√Always try to get the best-quality merchandise for the least money. Take bids on orders for stationery and supplies. Get more than one quotation on the cost of insurance coverage and the use of an answering service.

√Don't send books by first-class mail when book rate will do. Seek other means of shipping large lots of books.

√Use public transportation whenever possible to cut down on the expense of driving and parking your own car.

√When buying advertising space, look into multiple-day bargain rates. Evaluate circulation numbers and readership interests to assure yourself of getting the best response for your advertising dollar.

√Whenever possible, do all your own work. Never hire someone to deliver books when you can do it yourself. Don't pay to get letters typed when you can peck them out. Be both boss and slave.

√Pay your bills as you go along. You'll save carrying charges and keep your credit rating in top shape for the day you may want to ask for a loan.

√Collect payment for books sold at the time of delivery. This policy saves you the expense of billing and eliminates the risk of not being paid.

√Keep an emergency fund of cash in reserve. You never know when an estate may come on the market and you'll need ready cash to buy good books. Keep your reserve fund in an account that pays interest. Keep only a minimum of working cash in your checking account.

√Try to sell directly to customers rather than letting your stock go out on consignment. Books waiting to be sold are tying up cash. The consignment dealer charges a percentage of the sale and cuts into your profits.

√Try to make do with what simple equipment you have rather than investing in an expensive office layout and a new automobile.

HOW TO SET UP A
LOW-OVERHEAD
OFFICE

It isn't necessary to spend a lot of money on a solid oak desk or an electric typewriter to get started in the book scouting business. An office can be as simple as a table and chair moved into a corner. Letter writing, billing, and bookkeeping can all be done on this table. Your salesroom can be the trunk of your car or even a briefcase if you travel by bus. All you need is a place to carry the stock you have for sale that day.

If you intend to hang out a shingle in front of your house announcing that you're in business, make certain that your business activity falls within the purview of local zoning regulations. If you are renting, check your lease.

Such simple office requirements as those described here may sound like a very small start, and that is exactly the way it should be. You cut your risk of loss

Book scouts don't need an elaborate office or a shop to sell from. A salesroom can be the trunk of your car.

when you cut the amount you have tied up in business. If you find, after a few weeks' trial, that you do not like being a book scout, you can always move that table back to another part of the room, and you won't be out much but your time. If you do like book scouting, you can always expand. In either case, you are never going to need an elaborate office.

It is not a good idea to quit a steady job with the idea of going into book scouting full time until after you've tried it. First, work at being a book scout in your spare time for a while to see how you like it and whether you can support yourself, which takes quite a lot of doing. If you are a roaring success, you can always quit your other job or work at it part time if possible.

In addition to a table and chair setup for your office, there are other pieces of equipment you should consider if you want to operate to the best advantage.

OPTIONAL EQUIPMENT

A Telephone

Your telephone will pay for itself by saving you time when making appointments and checking out book-supply sources. Though there is no substitute for personal calls on customers, some types of transactions can be handled just as well by phone. For example, orders for supplies can be phoned in. Advertising copy can be phoned to newspapers. Meeting dates, sale hours, and other information can be requested by phone. But when you have a book to sell, take it directly to your customer. A customer can reject a book a lot easier on the phone than when it's presented in person.

After your business is well established and customers have begun calling you to make requests or answer ads, you may want to hire an answering service. If you miss a call while you are out scouting because your phone is unanswered, that customer may not call again; but if buyers can leave a message, you may make a sale. If you decide to try an answering service, be sure to take two bids on cost before awarding a contract.

An alternate choice to an answering service is an automatic phone-answering system that records messages from callers. Some systems even allow you to check messages from an outside line. This feature could save you time and trips. But unless you deal with customers by phone quite often and are missing sales because you are missing calls, don't rush out and buy a recording unit. Some cost several hundred dollars.

A Typewriter

Your correspondence, bills, and orders will have a more businesslike appearance if they are typed rather than written by hand. This does not mean that you should go out and buy an elaborate or even a new typewriter. Even an old manual machine will serve you well to type a few letters. Just remember to keep your type clean and to have a good ribbon in the machine.

Business Stationery

Conservative, personalized, business stationery with your name, address, and phone number (including area code) printed on the letterhead is versatile enough to serve several purposes. Bills and receipts as well as letters can all be typed on this paper. Select heavy white stock, size 8½ by 11 inches, with black type. Envelopes and business cards should be printed in matching type.

Although this stationery will mean an outlay of

some of your working capital, it is as important as any piece of office equipment you may purchase. This paper, with its official letterhead, is your representative in the mail. A businesslike letter can mark the difference between an amateur and a professional. Order at least 500 sheets of paper, 400 envelopes, and 1,000 business cards. You will save money and the time it takes to reorder.

Offer your business card at every opportunity. The card you hand to one prospective customer today may get handed on and bring you another customer tomorrow.

A Pocket Calculator

Dime stores and drugstores are now selling perfectly accurate pocket calculators for just a few dollars. If you can possibly afford one, you should consider buying a calculator. This little instrument can be a useful tool in helping you do your bookkeeping, compute taxes, figure interest rates, and add up profits. If you buy one, get a pocket model you can carry with you when you go out on a book search. With your calculator in hand, you can make instant, on-the-spot financial decisions.

Record Books

For tax purposes, you must keep accurate records of your business income and expenditures. Buy a small book you can carry with you in your pocket to record expenses. It is easy to forget bus fare or parking charges if you don't write them down when you pay the money out. All out-of-pocket expenses incurred by you that are directly connected with your business may be considered for tax deductions.

In addition to an expense book, you will also need a bookkeeping ledger. If you are not familiar with bookkeeping methods, you may want to seek help with this aspect of your business. This is discussed later in this chapter.

Supplies to Restore and Repair Books

A part of your work will probably include some cleaning and slight repair of the books you buy. The few simple supplies that are needed and instructions for use are covered completely in Chapter 5.

A Daily Engagement Book

A small pocket calendar and date book, with spaces for notes and appointments, is almost a must for keeping your life straight. You'll want to record daily appointments, meetings, notes of book fairs, auctions, book sales and shows, and other important dates. If you use your pocket engagement book faithfully, you will never trip up and make two appointments for the same hour.

Book-Trade Periodicals

Subscribe to as many magazines dealing with the book trade as you find helpful and can afford. The cost of a subscription may soon be erased by the sales leads you gain from the want lists in the periodical. If you can't afford to subscribe, do try to read copies at your local library. A partial list of useful publications appears in Chapter 9.

An Automobile

Use of a car is almost essential if you are living in a rural area where adequate public transportation is not available. In any area, a car will help you transport large numbers of books to and from sales, auctions, club meetings, and appointments. Consult your automobile insurance broker or agent about the amount of legal liability insurance you will need to cover you for property damage or bodily injury to others. Such coverage is mandatory in most states.

A Post Office Box

A post office box may be a wise investment if you buy or sell a number of books by mail. A box sometimes offers faster service and greater security than home delivery if you have an outside mailbox. Security is especially important if you are receiving many checks in the mail. However, if you don't do business by mail, don't invest in a box.

The Right Clothing

The right kind of clothes to wear when contacting customers should be considered an important part of your investment program. Proper clothing can give you an advantage in a sales situation. A neatly and conservatively dressed person looks businesslike and professional. You don't need to go out and buy a whole new wardrobe to create this impression. One well-made dark outfit will serve all your needs. The importance of appearance when making sales calls is also mentioned in Chapter 7.

These basic supplies for starting your business all cost money, but a frugal person can buy many of them from inexpensive sources. Used equipment will often do just as well as new. And as has already been suggested, many of the items mentioned can wait until your business is well established.

THE IMPORTANCE OF
KEEPING GOOD FILES

Keeping good files can be your wisest investment of time. The value of files will become evident as soon as you begin to use them. Good files help you buy wisely and sell profitably. Files should be distinguished from records in this way: Bookkeeping records are maintained for tax and budget purposes, whereas files help promote an efficient and profitable business. Most book scouts find two different types of files helpful—a small card file and a larger folder file. Both are discussed here.

Card Files and What to Include
in Them

A card file with the names, addresses, and telephone numbers of customers is a valuable sales tool. In addition to the basic information already mentioned, other useful data that each customer card might include are as follows:

√Type of book the customer is interested in.

√Price range customer will consider.

√Customer's past purchases, including type of book, sale price, and your profit.

√How customer contact was made. (This information could lead you to other customers.)

In addition, your personal comments about dealing with this customer will help you when trying to sell to him or her in the future. Such notes might run something like this:

"Contact at home evenings."

"Prefers to be billed."

"Will buy reading copies."

"Sometimes buys cookbooks for sister's collection."

The more notes you have about each customer, the more personal you can make your service. Personal service leads to more frequent sales.

Folder Files and What to Include in Them

Folder files are useful for storing larger papers, booklets, and notes of greater length. To start with, you can get by with a few old folders and a cardboard box to keep them upright, but as your business grows, you should consider a small drawer file. Used-office-equipment stores frequently have this type of file for sale at a reasonable price. Folders in some of the following designations will probably prove useful.

Sales Records. These records are in addition to your bookkeeping accounts. They include personal notes and observations on what type of book sells well in certain areas or at certain times of the year, what type of book sells for the most profit, and what kind of book sells the most readily.

Books on Consignment. You may wish to sell some of your books on consignment with auction houses. For this service, the auction house will claim a percentage of the profits, but they may also get a better price than you would on your own. Your files should contain complete records of all books out on consignment, including receipts for the delivery of these books.

Book-Buying Notes. You will find it useful to keep notes on outlets where you have had good luck finding books. Notes of this type might look something like this:

Outlet A: "Good values at First Baptist Church December bazaar."

Outlet B: "Call Carl Waverly for books after his January overseas trip."

Outlet C: "Check this shop for markdown
           on reading copies after first of year."

   You should also keep notes concerning outlets you
are wary of trading with again. Such notes might look
something like this:

Outlet A: "Have found plates missing in
           illustrated volumes."
Outlet B: "Books are overpriced."
Outlet C: "Promised deliveries usually
           late."

Catalogues and Sales Lists.   Catalogues for dealer sales
and auction houses make valuable reference material.
Book condition will be described and prices listed.
Although prices are constantly changing and depend
upon the condition of a book, you can learn general
price range from this type of material. Keep catalogues
and study them.

News Clippings and Magazine Articles.   Even outdated
news sometimes offers information you may want to
refer to again. And articles about books that may not
interest you today may offer the information you will
seek tomorrow. Save valuable articles in files for future
reference.

Correspondence.   Save all letters from customers. Letters
may prove valuable for tax records, offer information

leading to future sales, and even lead to new customers. Studying back correspondence can help you repeat successes and avoid mistakes.

HOW TO KEEP YOUR BUSINESS SIMPLE AND LEGAL

The minute you buy your first book and resell it, you're in business. And the minute you're in business, there are forms to file and taxes to pay. You must never neglect or skip over any legal business requirements if you hope to stay out of trouble. However, there are some perfectly *legal* steps you can take to cut down on your paperwork and fee paying.

Whenever practical, a book scout can cut down on business reporting by working under the following guidelines:

Work Alone

Don't form partnerships or take on employees unless you absolutely have to. A one-person business or a business operated by a husband-and-wife team is known as a *sole proprietorship*. If you want to save yourself hours of paperwork and legal complications and cut your tax reporting down, make your business a sole proprietorship. This category is the least regulated of any type of business arrangement.

Work Under Your Own Name

Although it might fulfill a lifelong ambition to call your business "The Backwoods Book Scout" or some other such thing, naming your business that way means that in some areas, you must file a Fictitious Business Name Statement with the county clerk and pay a filing fee. Where required, you may also have to run a statement in the local newspaper announcing that you will be doing business under a fictitious name. Newspaper ads cost money, so you should check into state law before using anything other than your own name.

You may complicate the work of setting up your business still further if you call yourself a corporation. You cannot legally use this title unless you incorporate. When you incorporate, more papers must be filed. In most instances, it is best to work under your own name.

Work on a Cash Basis

Always pay for purchases in full at the time you collect them, and whenever possible, collect for books sold when you deliver them.

Keep your fees and taxes paid up quarterly.

Although you save on paperwork by being a sole proprietor, you are also solely responsible for debts. If you get into financial trouble and go deeply into debt, as sole proprietor, you can lose your business and other privately accumulated assets as well. Pay up as you go along, and don't gamble by going into debt.

REPORTS YOU WILL BE
REQUIRED TO FILE

By working alone (keeping your business a sole proprietorship), working under your own name, and working on a cash basis as much as possible, you will cut paperwork and report filing to a minimum. However, you must still file the following tax forms and reports:

√Federal Income Tax Form 1040

√Quarterly Estimated Tax Form 1040-ES

√Social Security Tax Schedule SE (All self-employed persons must file this form.)

√Schedule C—Profit or Loss From Business or Profession (Sole Proprietorship) Attach to Form 1040

In addition to these reports, in some places where there is a state sales tax, you must apply for a sales permit from the State Board of Equalization and pay tax on all sales. The state law determines whether your sales tax returns are due monthly, quarterly, or yearly. In some states, you pay tax only on intrastate sales. Others also require a sales license. Check your local laws.

If you do *not* hire employees, you will *not* need a Federal Employer Identification Number. Your Social Security number will act as your business identification number on all forms.

All these requirements may sound like a lot of

paperwork, but they are nothing compared to the mountain of work you can get into if you employ people or go into a partnership or joint venture.

You'll come out all right if you file tax reports in full and on time. Just because you are selling out of the trunk of your car and your office consists of an old table and chair does not mean that you can fail to comply with government regulations.

WHERE TO FIND HELP
AND ADVICE

Coping with the complexities of tax reports, bookkeeping, insurance coverage, and money management can be pretty overwhelming, but there are places where people offer help and advice. Some of this help is even free. Just because you've chosen to have a go at running a business by yourself doesn't mean that you shouldn't seek advice from experts who can help you avoid some of the business world's legal and financial pitfalls.

Both individual states and the federal government maintain agencies to offer personal assistance to small businesses. A list of those agencies follows.

United States Small Business
Administration

Local offices of the SBA offer advisory services and workshops to help with business problems. The SBA also produces a number of fine publications and some educational materials. Workshops are offered for very nominal fees, and most publications are free. In some areas, retired business executives act as advisors to answer questions personally.

United States Department of
Commerce

Census extracts, compiled and furnished by this office, can help you determine market areas. Information on educational levels of the population by area, obtainable from this office, can help you with sales. When you know where to find people who like to read and are interested in books, the job of selling them is much easier.

Chamber of Commerce

Your local chamber can furnish area statistics on commercial growth patterns and population increases and decreases. This information can be useful in establishing a market area.

United States Internal Revenue
Service

If you have difficulty completing your tax statements, you may benefit from the free help and advice offered by the IRS. You may seek assistance in any one of the following ways:

√Write your IRS District Director.

√Call IRS Information by toll-free telephone. The number for assistance in your area is listed in your yearly IRS Instruction Booklet.

√Go to your nearest IRS office for personal assistance.

Although the IRS will answer your questions and help you prepare your return, keep in mind that you alone are still responsible for the accuracy of your tax return and for paying the correct tax.

In addition to public agencies, you may at some time need the help and advice of professional advisors. It has already been mentioned that you may want to seek the aid of an accountant in setting up your books and that of an insurance agent when selecting automobile coverage if you are using a car for business. One other advisor you may find helpful is your local banker. A good relationship with a banker may prove useful in more than one way.

Although advised earlier that it is not a good idea to go into debt, there may come a time when you want to ask for a business loan if an estate or a large lot of books comes on the market that you cannot afford to buy outright. Your banker will advise you whether your financial position warrants the risk.

Your banker will also be able to explain the benefits that self-employed persons accrue when they open either an Individual Retirement Account (IRA) or a Keogh Plan. These plans allow you to deduct the amount contributed from your taxable income and to defer tax on the amount contributed and interest earned until you start withdrawing your money at any time between the ages of 59½ and 70½. If you are of an eligible age and not covered by any other employer-sponsored retirement plan, either one of these plans (depending on the size of your income) is a fine way for self-employed persons to provide for their retirement.

Use the business advice in this chapter when you need it, but don't let the details of taxes, bookkeeping, banking, and insurance spoil the challenge and fun of being a scout on the trail of a book.

The Tools
of the Trade

N O DOUBT BY NOW you are excited about trying your hand at book buying and anxious to see what kind of sales you can make. But before you head out for the marketplace, it would be wise to take the time to read these last few pages of book world facts. The terms, numbers, dates, sizes, and vocabulary presented here can do a lot to take the mystery out of book buying and can help ensure you a more profitable search among the book-lined shelves of the world.

Some rules never change. It is safe to say that the vocabulary of the book world is stable. For centuries, book talk and book lore have gone on virtually unchanged. When you have learned to use the tools of the trade that follow, you will have unlocked the doors of the old-book world.

ROMAN NUMERALS

The dates in many old books are written in Roman numerals. This practice began when Roman numerals were in common usage and is continued in some publishing even today.

The numerals X, V, C, and others look like letters instead of numbers, and for good reason. Roman letters were used in forming numbers until the tenth century.

Until you memorize the numbers that Roman numerals represent, publication dates in many old books will elude you. While you are learning, it is helpful to carry a small card with the key to values written on it. If you keep this card handy whenever you go out on a book search, you'll be able to decipher complicated looking dates. With a little practice, the card can be discarded, and you'll be on your own.

Here are the values of the symbols:

$$I = 1$$
$$V = 5$$
$$X = 10$$
$$L = 50$$
$$C = 100$$
$$D = 500$$
$$M = 1,000$$

Other numbers are formed from these basic letters by adding or subtracting the value of a symbol preceding or following another symbol. For example, the value of a symbol preceding one of greater value is subtracted: $IX = 9$; $XIV = 14$.

The value of a symbol following another of greater value is added on: $III = 3$; $XVI = 16$.

A bar over a letter indicates multiplication by 1,000: $\overline{V} = 5,000$; $\overline{X} = 10,000$.

Here are a few examples of publication dates:

$$MDCCLXXVI = 1776$$
$$MDXC = 1590$$
$$MDL = 1550$$
$$MDCCXXII = 1722$$

BOOK TERMS

The more you associate with people who love, sell, and collect books, the deeper you will delve into the specialized vocabulary they use. To list all the words relating to the book trade would take a volume in itself. Many terms are highly technical and would be of little use to beginning book scouts; therefore, only some of the more frequently used words are defined here.

ADDENDUM.   A supplement or appendix added to the text.

ADVANCE COPY.   Book copies sent out by the publisher to reviewers, critics, judges of book clubs, and chosen booksellers.

ADVERTISEMENTS.   Pages of advertising copy, often for other books by the same author and publisher, bound in at the end of a book.

ALL EDGES GILT.   Said of a book that has all three outer edges of the leaves gilded.

AMERICANA.   Books or pamphlets about America, North and South, its people and its history. In North America this term usually refers to books about the United States. Americana may be divided into subject divisions such as: discovery, exploration, settlement, the Revolution, the Civil War, the West, and others.

ANA.   An *ana* may be added to the name in a title when the material is about a particular author or subject. For example, books about the author O. Henry might be entitled O. Henryana. Books about America are referred to as Americana.

ANNUALS.   Books that are issued serially once a year. Some annuals are finely bound or similarly bound each year.

ANTIQUARIAN. Said of a book that is antique, very old. No age has ever been clearly defined.

ANTIQUE FINISH. A term used to describe the surface of paper that has a naturally rough finish.

ARMORIAL BINDING. A leather binding, either blind stamped or stamped in gilt, with a coat of arms, school crest, or heraldic crest.

AS ISSUED. A description used to define a book in its original condition.

ASSOCIATION COPY. A book that contains evidence that it was owned by the author or some famous person. Evidence may be a signature, bookplate, inscription, or a laid-in letter.

Books with coats of arms, school crests, or heraldic crests are on the want lists of collectors.

AUCTION. A public sale of books where single volumes and lots are sold to the highest competing bidder.

AUTHOR'S BINDING. Book copies bound to the author's order, usually for presentation to friends.

AUTOGRAPHED COPY. A book signed by the author and sometimes numbered.

BACKSTRIP. The back edge of a book along which sections are fastened together in binding. Modern books have springback binding, not fastened to the signatures.

BEVELED EDGES. Sloping or angled edges cut into a book's boards as a decorative measure.

BIBLIO. From the Greek term *biblion,* meaning "book" when used in combination with other words.

BIBLIOGRAPHER. A person who has expert knowledge of an author or a particular subject—may be an authority on recognizing first editions.

BIBLIOPHILE. A lover and collector of books.

BINDER'S BOARDS. The stiff, flat sheets of pasteboard used for the cover of a book.

BLANK LEAVES. Leaves without printing or illustration, usually found at the beginning and end of a book and at clearly marked divisions. A book loses value when these leaves have been removed.

BLIND STAMPED or BLIND TOOLED. An impression stamped or made with bookbinders' tools to create a bas-relief design on a book cover. The design is not gilded.

BLOCK BOOK. Picture books with pages printed from single wooden blocks or metal plates. This type of book preceded the invention of movable type.

BLURB. A slang term referring to a book jacket or publishing catalogue write-up about a book's content and author.

BOARD PAPER. The portion of the end paper that is pasted down on the inside of the front and back covers of a book. The paper is often of a different color or texture than the page stock.

BOARDS. Originally, the wooden sides of a book. Pasteboards were substituted in about the sixteenth century to reduce weight.

BOOK JACKET. A removable paper wrapper for a book. Some jackets are printed with advertising copy, illustrations, or the author's picture. Also called a DUST JACKET.

BOOKPLATE. A label usually affixed to one of the front end papers with the name of the owner of the book printed or written on it. Many early bookplates were hand-painted. Also known as an *ex libris,* meaning "from the library of."

BOOKWORM. The larva of an insect that eats holes in books. Also a slang expression referring to a person who is an avid reader.

BOSS. Protruding metal knobs, sometimes of gold or silver, fastened to the surface of the leather sides of a book and used by early binders to protect covers from wear. Some were later incorporated in decoration.

BREAKING-UP. To separate plates from a book for the purpose of selling them for framing. This practice greatly damages if not destroys a book.

BROADSHEET. An unfolded sheet of paper with printing on both sides.

BROADSIDE. An unfolded sheet of paper with printing on one side.

BUCKRAM. A coarse cotton, hemp, or linen cloth stiffened with glue and used to bind books.

CALFSKIN. A smoothly tanned hide of a calf used to bind books. May be dyed or left a natural shade of pale brown. Calf may be treated in a number of ways and may be further described as polished, sprinkled, mottled, diced, scored, or grained.

CANCEL. A leaf tipped into a book to replace original text.

CAP. The cap or headcap of a book is the top of the spine.

CARTOUCHE. An ornamental design, originally in the form of a scroll, used on title pages, maps, or at the beginning of a new chapter.

CASE BOUND. Said of a book built around a hardboard, not a paper wrap.

CASE/BOX. A box made to measure for the preservation of a book.

CATCHWORD. The first word on a new page, printed at the lower right-hand corner of the preceding page to aid in collation. Usually seen only in books printed before 1800.

CATHEDRAL BINDINGS. A term applied to binding decorated with Gothic or architectural motifs.

CHAIN MARKS. Lines running parallel with the grain, usually about one inch apart, in laid paper. These marks are made by the wire mesh at the bottom of the tray in which the paper is made. Often gives the paper a ribbed effect. Chain marks are sometimes imitated in machine-made papers.

CHAPBOOK. Books peddled on the street by "chapmen" or "chaps," popular from the seventeenth to the nineteenth centuries. These books usually contained folktales, lurid or sensational stories, or even ballads— were usually done on cheap paper with poor printing.

COATED STOCK. Paper having a glossy surface coating that produces a smooth finish.

COLLATION. To check the pages of a rare book, leaf by leaf, to make certain it is complete. Collation may be done using a copy certified perfect, using the table of contents, using page numbers or illustration list.

COLOPHON. An inscription at the end of a book giving details of production. The colophon may include the publisher's trademark or device. Most often found in early books that had no title pages. From the Greek word meaning "summit" or "finishing stroke."

COLOR PLATE. Originally referred to the hand-colored and tipped-in illustrations of a book. Now refers to plates in color, whether they are printed, engraved, lithographed, or hand-colored.

COMMISSION. Books published on commission are paid for by the author. The implication may be that the material was refused by a publisher as a bad risk. Some books paid for by the author are done by a VANITY PRESS.

CONDITION. One of the primary factors in pricing a book is its physical appearance and present state of preservation.

CONJUGATE LEAVES. The connecting leaves formed from a single sheet of paper. The leaves that belong to one another.

CONTEMPORARY. Bindings, end papers, plates, and inscriptions made in sympathy with the period of the book's publication.

COPYRIGHT PAGE. Usually the VERSO (back of) the title page. This page contains the date when the exclusive right of publication was granted by law. Information may also include the number of copies printed.

COVER. The binding of a book. The upper cover is the front, and the lower cover is the back side of the binding.

CRISP. A term used to describe book condition, meaning one with leaves not dulled by handling.

CROPPED. A book whose margins have been cut down. Cropping is usually done to allow for the binding machine. A book deeply cropped may have lost part of its printed text.

CUT. A term used to describe an illustration printed with the text.

DANDY ROLL. A wire cylinder used in machine papermaking to produce laid effects on the texture of the paper.

DECKLE EDGE. The rough or untrimmed edge of a page of handmade paper, formed where the pulp flows against the deckle, or edge, of the frame. Can be artificially produced in machine-made papers.

DEDICATION COPY. A copy of a book inscribed by the author to the person to whom the book has been dedicated.

DEFECTIVE. A cataloguer's term used to describe almost every degree of book damage. Most often refers to the exterior of a book.

DENTELLE. A French term meaning "lacework," usually referring to the lacy design around the inner edge of the cover of a book—usually done in gilt. Dentelle decoration may also be used on the outside of covers.

DEVICE. Printer's or publisher's mark found along with the colophon at the end of a book in books printed

Books with lacy dentelle and colorful endpapers are wanted by collectors, but they will also sell as gift items.

before 1500. Today the device is often found on the title page.

DIAPER. A binding decoration often in a crosshatched pattern of squares or triangles containing flower prints. May be blind or gilt embossed.

DICED. A term used by binders meaning a cover that has been ruled or stamped into a pattern of diamond squares. Calfskin is often diced.

DOUBLURE. An ornamental lining on the inner side of a book cover, not of paper but of leather, usually decorated.

DUST WRAPPER. A paper jacket wrapped around a book to protect the cover. Same as DUST JACKET or BOOK JACKET.

EARLY PRINTED. Books printed from 1600 to 1640. To be distinguished from INCUNABULA, or books printed in the fifteenth century.

EDGES. Refers to the three outer edges of the leaves of a book, which may be cut, uncut, trimmed, gilt, gauffered, sprinkled, or marbled.

EDITION. The number of copies of a book printed at any time or times from the exact same setting-up of type. An IMPRESSION includes the number of copies of a book of that edition printed at *one* time without the type or plates being removed from the press.

EDITIO PRINCEPS. From the Latin, meaning "first edition."

ELEPHANT FOLIO. A book with a page size of about 14 by 20 inches, often used in illustrated art books. In modern slang, these are referred to as furniture or cocktail-table books.

END PAPERS. The double folded leaves of paper, one-half of which is pasted to the inside of either the front or back cover of a book. The other half of the end paper forms the first or last page of the book. In some early books, the end papers were hand painted. In modern books they may be printed with maps, genealogical trees, or illustrations. End papers made of the same stock as the text are referred to as "own ends."

ENGRAVING. A term applied to any illustration or decoration made from a plate whose surface has been incised with a graver or burin. The plate was usually made of copper until about 1830, when steel began to be used.

ERRATUM. An error or mistake found after a book has been printed. Corrections are sometimes listed on a separate sheet and tipped into the book.

FACSIMILE. A copy or exact reproduction of an original.

FAIR MARKET VALUE. The price a book will sell for on the open market.

FEATHERED EDGE. A rough-cut edge of a page made to look like the deckle edge found in handmade paper. Feathering is sometimes accomplished by tearing paper along the edge of a steel comb.

FIRST EDITION. All copies of a book printed from the first set of plates. A minor change in type will result in a *first issue*. A second change will result in a *second issue*. Issues are created when deliberate textual changes are made. A STATE refers to a change made because of defective or broken type or other needs for repair during a press run.

FIRST SEPARATE EDITION. The first appearance of a book that had been printed with other material and is now printed alone.

FIRST TRADE EDITION. First printing of a work for trade distribution that had previously been printed in a limited edition or a private edition.

FLYLEAF. The free front end paper.

FOLIATION. The number of leaves of a book, as opposed to *pagination,* which is the number of pages.

FOLIO. A leaf numbered on the RECTO, or front. Also, a book approximately 17 by 22 inches in size made from book paper folded only once.

FONT (of type). The style of the letter and/or its size. A complete assortment of type of one size and face.

FORE-EDGE. The front edge of the pages of a book. A fore-edge painting is done by clamping a book in a partially fanned out position, then painting a scene in water color on the margin edge. The book is then closed and the edges gilded. The painting is then concealed while the book is closed and can only be seen when the book is again fanned open.

FORMAT. Refers to the general shape, style, and appearance of a book. Format includes size, binding, color, paper stock, design, and other physical features.

FOXED. Said of paper that is discolored or stained, usually with brownish-red spots.

FRONTISPIECE. The first illustration in a book. Often appears facing the title page. In many instances in older books, the frontispiece is a picture of the author. When

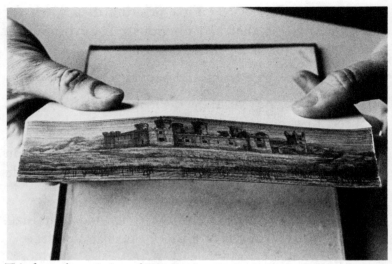
This fore-edge painting of Camelot is completely hidden when the book is closed. Good fore-edge paintings are difficult to find and costly.

plates are numbered in sequence, the frontispiece is seldom included.

GALLEYS. A proof taken of text on long strips of paper before type is locked into a frame. Galleys began to be used in the early part of the nineteenth century. They are prized by some collectors but they pose a problem in shelving and preservation.

GATHERING. A unit of a book formed when printed sheets have been folded to the size of a book. Also known as a *section,* QUIRE, or SIGNATURE.

GAUFFERED; GOFFERED; GOFFRED. Said of a book that has the fore-edge of its pages impressed with heated tools to make indented patterns.

GILDING. The edges of the leaves of many books are gilded. Usually the edges have been cut smooth, but in some rare French and English editions, the edges are gilded without first being cut smooth.

GOTHIC TYPE. The earliest type ever designed for German printers. Closely resembling the hand-drawn letters of early scribes, it is used today mostly for certificates, diplomas, and invitations. Also called *black letter.*

GRAIN. In papermaking, the direction in which most of the fibers lie. Paper will fold or tear straight with the grain.

GRANGERIZED. A book with a number of extra illustrations tipped in that were not part of the original printed volume.

GRAVY BROWNING. The margins of boards and pages of rebound books are sometimes colored with a water-color solution to fake the faint, browning tinge of age. This process is called gravy browning.

GUARD. A strip of paper or muslin bound into the spine of a book. The end sheet can be glued to this guard.

GUARDED. A guarded leaf or plate is one that is put into a book by pasting its inner edge to a prepared stub. Also referred to as TIPPED IN.

GUTTER. The blank space or inner margin of a book from the binding to the printed area.

HALF BOUND. A book with leather binding on the spine, a portion of the sides, and corners, with cloth or paper over the remainder. Also known as *half leather*.

HEADBAND. In modern books the headband is a ribboned strip pasted to the back of the top of the binding to add strength and protection to this area. In early binding, the headband was worked over leather or cord and fastened inside the top of the spine as part of the process of binding.

HEADPIECE. A printed or engraved decoration at the head of a chapter or division of a book.

HINGE. The junction where the cover and backstrip of the binding meet and bend.

HINGED CATCH. A clasp used for fastening the front and back covers of a book together at the fore-edge. A catch may be made of silver and even encrusted with jewels.

HORAE or BOOK OF HOURS. A collection of prayers for private devotional use at the canonical offices of the Roman Catholic Church.

HORNBOOK. A tablet fitted with a handle containing the alphabet, simple numbers, elements of spelling, or the Lord's Prayer. The writing was protected by a thin plate of translucent horn. Hornbooks were used in rudimentary education from the sixteenth to early eighteenth centuries. Authentic examples are very rare.

ILLUMINATED. To be decorated by hand. Early manuscripts were elaborately illuminated. During the first half century of printing, it was still common to hand decorate the first letter of a paragraph.

ILLUSTRATIONS. Drawings, paintings, woodblock prints, engravings, etchings, and photographs included in a book to illustrate the text.

IMPERFECT. Used to describe a book with damage to the interior parts.

IMPRESSION. The number of copies of an edition printed at one time.

INCUNABULA. From the Latin, meaning "swaddling clothes—things in cradle," and refers to books produced in the infancy of printing, usually before the year 1500.

INLAID. Said of bindings with colored leathers stuck into the main binding in elaborate mosaic designs.

IN PRINT. A book that is still available from the publisher.

INSCRIBED COPY. A book with a message inscribed in it by the author.

INTAGLIO. A design that is sunken below the surface. The design may be die cut, carved, or engraved.

INTERLEAVED. A book bound with blank leaves alternating with printed leaves.

JAPON VELLUM. Pale cream-colored paper with a glossy surface. It is usually rather stiff like vellum and

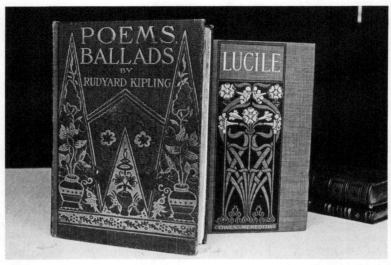
Old books with heavy intaglio on the covers make colorful collector's items.

is used for deluxe editions. Japon is an imitation of a very costly handmade paper from Japan.

JOINTS.   The exterior junction of the spine of a volume with its sides. HINGES refers to interior junctions.

JUVENILES.   A publisher's term referring to children's books.

JUVENILIA.   Material done by a writer in youth.

LABEL.   Lettering pieces used by binders that are glued to the spine of a book to indicate title and author.

LAID PAPER.   Paper made by hand. When held to the light, chain lines may be distinguished.

LAYOUT. The drawing, sketch, or pasteup of a proposed printed piece.

LEAF. A sheet of paper, the two sides of which are pages of a book.

LEVANT. Leather made from Levantine goatskins tanned with leaves of the sumac tree. Also known as *Morocco leather.*

LIMITED EDITION. Any edition that is limited to a stated number of copies. May be numbered and signed by the author.

LIMP. A binding without boards. Vellum, cloth, and suede are the most commonly used materials for limp books.

LINING. A cloth end paper, often silk, and most frequently used in suede books.

LIST PRICE. The original published price of a book.

LOOSE. A cloth book that is weakened at the hinges and has partially loosened end papers.

MADE-UP COPY. An imperfect copy of a book with missing leaves or plates that has had these missing pieces tipped in to make it complete. New leaves are occasionally supplied from a later edition.

MARBLED PAPER. Paper that is colored in a variegated pattern like marble. Used for end papers and to cover the outside of the boards of a book. Marbled paper was first made by transferring blobs of oil paint, floated on a gum solution, to the flat surface of a piece of paper that had been dampened with alum water and lowered onto the colors. Other designs were made by stirring the blobs of paint with a feather. This design was known as QUILLING or *feathering*. These patterns were later imitated in print.

MARGINS.   The white margins of a page. The top is referred to as the head and the lower margin as the tail. The inner margin is that nearest to the fold of the paper or the back of the book, and the outer margin is nearest the fore-edge.

MEZZOTINT.   A method of engraving on a copper or steel plate done by scraping or polishing part of a roughened surface to produce an impression of light or shade.

MINIATURE.   Very small books; in the technical sense, those measuring less than three inches in height.

MINT.   Term used to describe a book in flawless condition and the most sought-after by collectors.

MISBOUND.   A book with a leaf, leaves, or an entire signature misplaced.

MISPRINT.   A book with words or page numbers printed in error.

MONOGRAPH.   A book dealing in only one subject or part of one subject.

MOUNTED.   Said of engravings or other illustrations pasted down or lightly attached to a leaf of a book.

NO DATE. A term used to describe a book for which research has failed to establish an approximate date of publication.

NOT SUBJECT TO RETURN. A term used by an auctioneer when a normal guarantee on a book purchased is suspended.

OCTAVO. A book made by folding a book sheet into eight leaves or sixteen pages. Usually about 6 by 9 inches in size.

OFFPRINT. A section of a longer piece, run off and folded and stapled to make a short brochure. Offprints are usually distributed privately to the author's friends and are rarely offered for sale except as a collector's item.

OFFSET (or SET-OFF). The accidental transfer of ink from one printed page to another. May be caused by the book's being bound before the ink was properly dry.

ONLY. A qualifying term used to describe a book as having ten plates (only) or a set of books as five volumes (only), meaning that the book or series is incomplete.

ORIGINAL STATE. Used to describe books in their original condition, with wrappers preserved.

OUT OF PRINT. This means that no copies of a book are available from the publisher and implies that only secondhand copies are available. The book is no longer being reprinted.

OVERHANG COVER. A book cover that is larger in size than the pages it encloses. A *flush cover* is the same size as the pages it encloses.

PAGE. The single side of a leaf of a book.

PAMPHLET. A small booklet or brochure occupying fewer pages than would make a book. Pamphlets are always unbound.

PARCHMENT. The inner portion of the split skin of a sheep—not tanned but prepared with lime.

PASTE ACTION. The staining of endpapers by the paste used for attaching them to the boards.

PERIODICAL PRINTING. The printing of a book in serialized form in a magazine or newspaper.

PICA. A printer's unit of measurement. One pica equals 1/6 of an inch.

PIRATED EDITION. A term applied to an edition of a book produced and marketed without the authority of, or payment to, the author.

PLATE-MARK. An impression made in a leaf of paper by the edge of a metal engraving plate used in the illustrating process.

PLATES. Term used to describe an illustration printed separately from the text. Illustrations printed on text pages are called CUTS.

POINT. An identifying characteristic that determines the value of a book. A statement cut or altered, broken type, and other peculiarities are all points that determine the priority of an issue. Also a printer's unit of measurement. There are 12 points to a PICA, 72 points to an inch.

PRESENTATION COPY. A book inscribed to a particular person and given as a gift by the author.

PRIVATE PRESS. A privately owned press run by a printer who is usually more interested in fine book production than in profit. Does not include university presses.

PROOFS. The first trial of set type. Proofs are usually run on special paper (long galley sheets) and are also known as GALLEY PROOFS.

PROVENANCE. The history of a book's previous owners. Provenance is interesting in proportion to the interest of the previous owners.

QUARTER BOUND. A book with leather spine and a small width of overlap on either cover—has no protective leather corners.

QUARTO. A book made by folding a book sheet twice to make four leaves. Usually measures about 9 by 12 inches.

QUILLING. An end paper pattern. See MARBLED PAPER.

QUIRE. A section of a book. Synonymous with GATHERING or SIGNATURE.

RARITY. Refers to availability of a book. The degrees of rarity are as follows: *Absolute Rarity*—Any book printed in a very small edition with a total number surviving known to be very small. *Relative Rarity*—Any book surviving in small quantity, plus a public demand. *Temporary Rarity*—A book that is scarce because of an inadequate supply of copies on the market through a temporary shortage. *Localized Rarity*—Books sought after outside the area of their original circulation.

READING COPY.   A book that is not in collector's condition, but definitely readable.

REBACKED.   Said of a book that has had the backstrip of the original binding replaced.

REBOUND.   Said of a book that has had the entire original binding replaced.

RECASED.   A book that has become shaken and has been taken out of its covers and reglued, resewed, and resettled in them more firmly is said to be recased.

RECTO.   The right-hand page of an open book, usually carrying an odd page number.

RELATIVE HUMIDITY.   The amount of water vapor present in the atmosphere, as compared with the amount of moisture the air could contain at the same temperature. Important in the storage of books.

REMAINDERS.   Books unsold by their publisher. Usually sold to a wholesaler or bookseller who markets them at a reduced price.

REMARGINED.   Said of a book that has had one or more of its three outer margins of a leaf restored. A book is *extended* if the inner margin only is restored. A book is *inlaid* if all four margins have been renewed.

REMBOITAGE. The transferring of a book from its own binding to one more elegant or, alternately, transferring into a superior binding a text more interesting than the original.

REPRINT. A new edition or a new impression made from the same setting-up of type.

RESERVE PRICE. The set price below which a seller at an auction refuses to go.

REVIEW COPY. A copy of a book sent out before publication by the publisher to certain persons to review.

RUBBED. A leather or cloth binding that is worn, scuffed, or chafed.

RUBRIC. A large and intricately designed capital letter at the beginning of the first word of a chapter. In early manuscripts, the rubrics were often elaborate paintings. The predominant color used in these paintings was red, and they took their name from this feature.

SCARCE. Said of a book that is hard to find but not necessarily rare or exceptionally valuable.

SCOUT. A person who scouts out scarce and rare books for dealers and collectors. Also known as a *runner*.

SCUFFED. Said of a binding that is deeply rubbed or scratched.

SECOND EDITION. A book printed for the second time from a new set of plates.

SELF COVER. A book cover that is of the same-weight paper as the inside text pages. Early manuscripts were sometimes bound this way, as well as modern, inexpensive editions.

SEWED. A method of binding the signatures of a book together with thread.

SHAVED. The edges of the leaves of a book have been trimmed off, usually the whole margin has been shaved, and the outer edge of some letters may have been touched. The text is still readable.

SHORT COPY. Text that has been severely cut down by the binder.

SIGNATURE. The name given to a large printed sheet after it has been folded to the required size to make a section of a book. The term was originally derived from a letter placed at the bottom of the first leaf of each section as an aid to the binder in assembling the signatures in proper sequence.

SIZING. That property of paper that relates to its resistance to penetration by liquids. Pages are said to be sized when they have been coated with a glutinous wash.

SLIP CASE. A box made to hold a book. Usually the back of the spine is visible when the book is placed inside. Gift editions often come with a slip case.

SPINE. The back or backbone of a bound book. The spine is the part of the book that is visible as it stands closed on the shelf.

SPRINKLED. Bindings that are colored with small specks or spots are said to be sprinkled.

SQUARE. A term used to refer to the inside edge of the covers of a book that project beyond the leaves.

STAMPED. Refers to covers or pages impressed with a design.

STATE. That part of an edition that is different because of a change in type through an accidental break.

STILTED. Said of a book that has unusually deep projection of covers beyond the edges of the leaves. Stilting is deliberately used when a small book is bound to range in size with larger books on a shelf.

STRIKE THROUGH. The penetration of ink through paper.

SUNNED. Said of leather covers that are faded from the sun. Most often seen on exposed spines.

TAIL PIECE. A symbol or design indicating the end of a chapter or paragraph. In newspaper articles, the number 30 is used.

TEXT. The body copy of a page or book.

THREE DECKER. A book published in three separate volumes. Sometimes found in nineteenth-century novels.

TIPPED IN. A printed slip or illustration pasted into a book after it has been bound.

TISSUES. Tissue paper tipped in or loosely inserted opposite an illustration to absorb the offset of ink.

TITLE PAGE. The page at the beginning of a book that contains the title, subtitle, the author's name, and sometimes a short quotation.

TOOLED. Said of a binding that has been decorated with a hand impressing tool. When done without ink, it is called BLIND TOOLING.

TREE CALF. Said of calf binding that has been stained with copperas and pearl ash to create a design that resembles a tree.

TRIMMED. The evening of the roughly cut edges of a book. Usually done on a machine.

UNBOUND. A book or pamphlet not in binding. If the volume has never been bound, it will be described by the words *as issued*.

UNCUT. A book with the pages intact and the edges of the leaves without trimming. The edges are as issued. Most modern books have all edges cut.

UNOPENED. A book in which the leaves have not been severed by a paper knife.

VANITY PRESS. A press that prints books on commission for a fee. Usually the books are not a good risk for a publisher, so the author must pay to have them printed.

VELLUM. The skin of a calf, lamb, or young goat that has not been tanned but has been treated with lime. The leather is usually an off-white color. Most very early manuscripts were written on vellum. For binding, vellum was commonly used in the sixteenth and seventeenth centuries.

VERSO. The left-hand page of a book, usually carrying an even page number. Also the back of the title page, usually carrying the copyright date.

VIGNETTE. An illustration in which the edges shade gradually away until they blend into the unprinted paper.

WATERMARK. A distinguishing mark made in handmade paper that might include the maker's initials, name, or device.

WATERSTAINED. A book discolored by water.

WOODCUT. A woodcut is carved with a knife along a plank. A wood engraving is cut with a graver or burin on the cross section of the wood. In modern usage, *woodcut* refers to any illustration printed from wood as distinct from a print made from a metal plate.

WRAPPERS. The paper covers of a book. The paper is often marbled in antiquarian books.

YAWNING. A book that fans open and will not stay firmly closed between its covers is said to be yawning. This defect is found most often in miniature volumes that are too light to stay shut of their own weight.

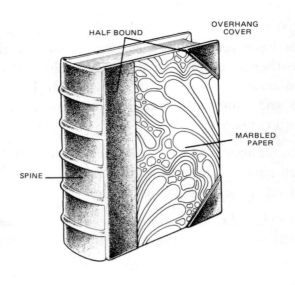

HALF BOUND

OVERHANG COVER

MARBLED PAPER

SPINE

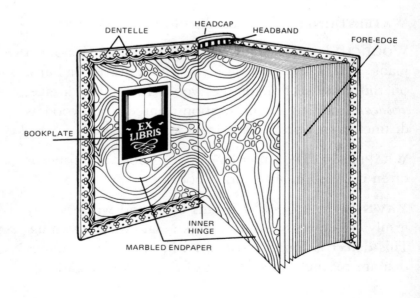

DENTELLE

HEADCAP

HEADBAND

FORE-EDGE

EX LIBRIS

BOOKPLATE

INNER HINGE

MARBLED ENDPAPER

BOOK-TRADE
PERIODICALS

Magazines for and about the book trade can prove to be a gold mine of information for book scouts. Although subscription rates to many of these magazines may seem costly, the customer leads they supply and the books they list for sale can, when followed up, lead to profits that will more than cover the rates.

All the periodicals listed next may not be valuable to every scout. Usefulness depends upon what type of leads you are looking for. Check your local library to see if copies are available for study, or write and request a sample copy of the periodical you are considering.

Although book-trade periodicals are printed in many countries throughout the world, only a sampling of those published in the United States are listed here:

Antiquarian Bookman: AB Bookman's Weekly
P.O. Box AB
Clifton, New Jersey 07015

This weekly magazine for book collectors, booksellers, librarians, and historians lists book fairs, dealers, restoration specialists, and books wanted and for sale.

Book Arts
The Center For Book Arts
15 Bleeker Street
New York, New York 10012

Specializes in articles on bookbinding, book history, and technical book arts. Has no set publication date. Beginning scouts can learn a great deal about book quality from this publication.

Book Collector's Market
Box 50, Cooper Station
New York, New York 10003

Specializes in articles about marketing rare books; bimonthly.

Fine Print—A Review for the Arts of the Book
P.O. Box 7741
San Francisco, California 94120

A critical guide to fine limited editions currently being produced. Lists reviews of currently published books about books and such related book arts as topography, bookbinding, papermaking, and printing. Also lists a calendar of current book events. Published quarterly.

The Book-Mart
144 South Second Street (P.O. Box 243)
Decatur, Illinois 46733

Emphasis is on book collecting and used book trade. Discusses pricing, conservation, and history of books. Published monthly.

The Collector
P.O. Box 255
Scribner Hollow Road
Hunter, New York 12442

Auction reports and items of interest to historical manuscript collectors. Also emphasizes autograph collections. Free to regular buyers.

TAAB Weekly: The Library Bookseller
P.O. Box 239 W.O.B.
West Orange, New Jersey 07052

Lists booksellers, libraries, and collectors interested in buying and selling. Published weekly.

This list does not include those publications that specialize in hobbies, book-craft material, and antiques other than antiquarian books.

BOOK TRADE
REFERENCE BOOKS

The volumes listed here offer thousands of leads to collectors, publishers, dealers, bookshops, libraries, auction houses, book prices, books in print, and trade directories.

Although many of these books are too expensive for most book scouts to own outright, they can be found in the reference sections of many public libraries. See the *Guide to Reference Books,* published by The American Library Association, for a brief explanation of each book listed here:

American Book Prices Current
Columbia University Press
562 West 113th Street
New York, New York 10025

This is a fine summary of auction prices compiled from auction catalogues of the previous season. Good pricing source.

American Book Trade Directory
Published annually by R. R. Bowker Co.
Edited by The Jaques Cattell Press
1180 Avenue of the Americas
New York, New York 10036

This lists book outlets, including book wholesalers and retailers, clubs, libraries, and publishers, in American and Canadian cities. Good lead for book-club buyers.

American Library Directory
Published by R. R. Bowker Co.
1180 Avenue of the Americas
New York, New York 10036

This directory lists 28,000 American and Canadian libraries and gives information about large library collections. Good lead for special-collection buyers.

Bookdealers in North America
Published by Sheppard Press Ltd.
Post Office Box 42
Russell Chambers
Covent Garden
London WC2E8AX England

Here is an extensive list of secondhand- and anti-quarian-book dealers in the United States and Canada. Useful in book searches and book sales.

Bookman's Price Index
Edited by Daniel F. McGrath, Curator of Rare Books, Duke University
Gale Research Company—Book Tower
Detroit, Michigan 48226

An annual guide to the values of rare and other out-of-print books and sets of periodicals. A good pricing source.

First Printings of American Authors (4 vols.)
Gale Research Company—Book Tower
Detroit, Michigan 48226

Gives illustrated facsimiles of title page and text pages. Photographs of bindings show highlights of important features of a book. Good source for checking copy authenticity.

Merle Johnson's American First Editions
R. R. Bowker Co.
1180 Avenue of the Americas
New York, New York 10036

Here are American first editions listed by author. Most copies of this book are old and well worn, indicating the value of the information contained.

Used Book Price Guide (2 vols.)
Price Guide Publishers
525 Kenmore Station
Kenmore, Washington 98028

This lists sale prices of rare, scarce, and used books. A useful comparative guide.

Also of great value in pricing are individual dealer and auction catalogues. Prices may be misleading unless they are carefully interpreted. Catalogues provide a level or a general idea of the trend of prices, but the condition of a volume sets its true value. The abbreviated style these catalogues use cannot be expected to give the reader a clear description of condition.

BOOKSELLERS' ABBREVIATIONS

ABAA	Antiquarian Booksellers' Association of America
ABC	American Book Prices Current
Abr.	Abridged
A.e.g.	All edges gilt
A.l.s.	Autograph letter, signed
Bd.	Bound
Bdg.	Binding
Bds.	Boards

Bib.	Bible
Bibliog.	Bibliography
Bk.	Book
C. & p.	Collated and perfect
Ca.	Circa
Cat.	Catalogue
Cent.	Century
Cf.	Calf
Cl.	Cloth
Col(d).	Color(ed)
Comp.	Compiled
Cond.	Condition
Cont.	Contemporary
Dec.	Decorated
D.j.	Dust jacket
Doc.	Document
D.s.	Document, signed
D.w.	Dust wrapper
Ed.	Edited
Edn.	Edition
Endp., e.p.	End paper
Engr.	Engraved

Ex-lib.	From the library
Facs.	Facsimile
Fol.	Folio, a size of book
Fp.	Frontispiece
G.e.	Gilt edges
G.l.	Gothic letter
G.t.	Gilt top
Gt.	Gilt
Hf. bd.	Half-bound
Ill.	Illustrated
Impft.	Imperfect
Inscr.	Inscribed
Intro.	Introduction
Ital.	Italic letter
Jt.	Joint
Leath.	Leather
Lge.	Large
Ll.	Leaves
L.s.	Letter signed
Ltd. edn.	Limited edition
Marg.	Margin
Mco, Mor.	Morocco

M.e.	Marbled edges
Ms(s)	Manuscript(s)
N.d.	No date of publication
N.p.	No place of publication
O.p.	Out of print
Orig.	Original
Pict.	Pictorial
P.I.R.A.	Printing Industry Research Association
Pol.	Polished
Port.	Portrait
Pp.	Pages
Pres.	Presentation copy
Pseud.	Pseudonym(ous)
Pt.	Part
Ptd.	Printed
Pub(d).	Publish(ed)
R.e.	Red edges
Repd.	Repaired
Rev.	Revised
Rom.	Roman letter
Sgd.	Signed

Sig.	Signature
Sm.	Small
Sp.	Spine
Spr.	Sprinkled
Sq.	Square
Swd.	Sewed
T.e.g.	Top edges gilt
T.l.s.	Typed letter, signed
T.p.	Title page
Unbd.	Unbound
V.d., v.y.	Various dates, years
Vell.	Vellum
V.g.	Very good (copy)
Vol(s).	Volume(s)
W.a.f.	With all faults
Wrs.	Wrappers
Y.e.	Yellow edges

SIZES OF BOOKS

A book's size is determined by the number of times a sheet of book paper is folded to form its leaves. The unit is not the page but the leaf. The size of a book sheet may vary, and subdivisions of these standard sizes may be produced. Size may also vary slightly according to how a book is trimmed or cut.

Some booksellers have dispensed with the use of these terms, which are becoming increasingly unfamiliar to many of their customers. Many catalogues describe book size in inches or centimeters. The following are the most frequently used book-size terms:

FOLIO. A sheet of book paper folded once to form a book of two leaves (four pages) about 17 by 22 inches in size. Abbreviated Fo.

QUARTO. Four leaves, eight pages, 9 by 12 inches, Qto., 4to.

OCTAVO. Eight leaves, sixteen pages, 6 by 9 inches, Oct., 8vo.

DUODECIMO. Twelve leaves, twenty-four pages, 5 by 7 inches, 12mo.

SEXTODECIMO. 16mo.

VICESIMO-QUARTO. 24mo.

TRICESIMO-SECUNDO. 32mo.

TERMS USED TO DESCRIBE BOOK CONDITION

Book condition is of primary importance to book scouts who hope to sell their purchases quickly and at a profit. If a book is worn, dirty, or stained, or is missing pages, it will generally be harder to sell. Age is no excuse for poor condition. Many books that have been given good care are still beautiful, even though they may be hundreds of years old. Book condition is usually graded on the following descending scale:

MINT. In new or original condition, as if freshly printed. Dust jacket will be crisp, bright, and unbent. Pages may be unopened.

FINE. May have been read, but has no marks, creases or blemishes on text or binding. Almost as new, but lacking new crispness.

VERY GOOD. Only a very few blemishes or marks of wear. May have owner's bookplate but not a written name.

GOOD. May have some small defects and the owner's name written in ink, but all pages are present.

FAIR. Readable, with all text intact. May be shaken, faded, browned, waterstained, thumbed, or soiled. May have some underlining or tears.

POOR. Missing pages, illustrations may have been removed, pieces of leaves torn out, end papers badly marked or missing. A badly maimed copy.

There are many trade expressions used to describe the condition of a book. Some of the more common of these are:

BINDING COPY. A volume with badly damaged covers but whose interior is in good condition and worth rebinding.

SECONDHAND COPY. Respectable condition but may be soiled.

READING COPY. A book that is intact and readable but not in collector's condition.

USED COPY. The grade between a reading and working copy.

WORKING COPY. The lowest grade of condition.

A visit to an auction will show you the astounding difference in the price two copies of the same book will bring if one is in fine condition and one is in only good condition.

Many booksellers are now stocking reading copies of books and are finding a demand for them among those people buying for speculation. Victorian novels with heavily decorated covers, now in demand by many new collectors, are often sold in "reading copy" condition.

WHERE TO SEE FINE COLLECTIONS

Visit great collections. There is probably no more valuable way to improve your knowledge of old books.

In almost any large city in the world, you will find museums and libraries housing fine book collections.

In addition, many universities, historical societies, and national associations support fine libraries.

Churches, private clubs, and private collectors sometimes display their treasures for commemorative events, to raise special funds, or to publicize an institution. Be alert for this kind of opportunity to see otherwise private collections.

The Library of Congress and the Smithsonian Institution Library, both in Washington, D.C., are well worth a trip.

Many bookshops encourage browsing.

Fine historical collections sometimes go on tour and can be seen in city museums. Admission price is usually very reasonable.

Take advantage of every chance you get to look at fine old books. You can learn a lot just by being around them.

How Old Books
Can Change Your Life

PEOPLE WHO BECOME BOOK SCOUTS very soon find that there are two sides to the book scouting story—the side the book scout sees and the one the scout's friends and family are left to live with. There are both positive and negative things to say about a book scout's job.

Here is a realistic look at the ledger:

Positive

1. Book scouts are never bored and never have time on their hands, because they are always in the process of hunting for books, buying books, and looking for book customers.

Negative

1. Book scouts frequently resolve to reform and do something besides talk about, think about, and look for books during their every waking minute; and then they wander off and disappear into the first bookshop they come to and forget all about their other responsibilities. This is certainly no boon to home life unless the whole family takes up book scouting.

2. Book scouts have a continual opportunity to learn, because the world of book trade is always changing.

2. There can be no letup in the study of book costs and current demands. To fall behind is to fail.

3. A book scout has the repeated pleasure of looking at, and buying, beautiful old books.

3. Book scouts must re-sell the books they buy even when they would like to keep them, or they are not in business.

4. A book scout can vacation anywhere and find something of interest to do, as every new city and town is fresh book-hunting territory.

4. Book scouts are never content to join their family in a vacation planned around such idle pursuits as golf or fishing. Book scouts never think of anything except what kind of book-hunting opportunities they will be able to uncover during their leisure time.

5. Book scouts never let their money sit around idle, not working for them. They always have their capital invested in books.

5. Book scouts rarely have enough money even to buy a new pair of shoes, because they have always just invested their last dime in some beautiful old book.

6. Book scouts can continually take part in the "joy of the chase" after old books.

6. Book scouts can be one step behind a book they've been tracking for weeks and yet lose it if another scout gets there first.

| 7. Book scouting is getting paid for doing something you enjoy. | 7. When you get stuck with a few books that won't resell, some of the fun goes out the window with the profit. |

But no matter how you choose to see the balance between pro and con in the life of a book scout, one fact remains certain—book scouts aren't like other people, and if you become a book scout, you will change too. Book scouting is a profession that can become an obsessive pursuit that will consume your time, blot out almost all other interests, and completely change your life.

Book scouting can lead you to gamble your last dime, cause you to become indifferent to the passing of time or even to the direction your feet may take you. Very soon, you won't even look the same, because even when book scouts try to appear neat, they frequently end up looking quite grubby. This can be blamed on the fact that musty attics, dank cellars, and dusty bookshelves are always looming up in front of them, promising hidden volumes and causing them to become oblivious to dirt and grime. But book scouts can't help being the way they are. They just don't think about unimportant things like time and appearance when they are on the trail of a book. And if you become a book scout, you will soon fall in with the same line of thinking.

The joy that book scouting will offer can be worth every cent you invest, every minute of time you spend, and every mile you walk. You'll find a new world in books, and you'll make new friends among book lovers who will share that world with you. And you'll be a happier, busier, and more interesting person than you have ever been before.

Wandering into an old bookshop where the aisles are narrow and books are stacked to the ceiling will be enough for you to get lost in that wonderful world where time doesn't matter, where the only sounds you hear are of the voices coming from the books.

Index